THE
GARLAND
OF
NATION-
SOULS

Complete Talks
at the
United Nations

SRI CHINMOY

Health Communications, Inc.
Deerfield Beach, Florida

Library of Congress Cataloging-in-Publication Data

Chinmoy, Sri, (date)
    The garland of nation-souls : complete talks at the United
Nations / Sri Chinmoy.
        p. cm.
    ISBN 1-55874-357-X
    1. Spiritual life. 2. United Nations—Miscellanea. 3. Peace—
Religious aspects. I. Title.
BL624.C467 1995
291.1'787—dc20   95-24013
                                                              CIP

Publisher: Health Communications, Inc.
            3201 S.W. 15th Street
            Deerfield Beach, Florida 33442-8190

Cover design by Andrea Perrine-Brower

CONTENTS

▨ 2

Spiritual Awakening: Journey to Our Oneness-Heart

3
Secrets of the Inner Life

6

Meditation: Language of the Soul

Prayerfully and gratefully I am dedicating
The Garland of Nation-Souls
to the world-illumining Soul of the
United Nations.

Sri Chinmoy

The United Nations: Heart-Home of the World-Body

"This meeting of ours has been most essential. Your message and mine are the same. When we both leave this world, you and I, we will meet together."

Pope Paul VI
March 22, 1972

"I'm very grateful for your visit. God bless you and all your contemplative activities."

Pope John Paul II
October 14, 1987

The United Nations:
Leader of the World-Family

There are many ideals that the United Nations can teach us how to share. If we do not share with others what we have and what we are, we are bound to feel unsatisfied, no matter what we achieve and what we grow into. Today I would like to speak about the ideal of the world-family.

Each nation is unique in its own way. Each nation has achieved something special, at least for itself. When a nation is ready to feel that other nations are an extension of its own being, when a nation becomes aware that all nations belong to one family, one source, and have one common goal, then that particular nation can easily teach or share its lofty achievements. Each nation knows inwardly that satisfaction and perfection lie only in self-giving, not in displaying grandiose achievements or in hoarding capacities.

All nations are pilgrims, eternal pilgrims, walking along the same road, the road of eternity. On the way, some become tired and want to take rest. They do not have the inspiration to walk any farther. At that moment, if the nations that are ahead can feed and energize those that have fallen back, then the lagging ones can easily keep pace with the nations that are marching speedily.

If a strong nation feels that its progress will be slow if it helps a weak one, I wish to say that this is not true. If one nation encourages, inspires, feeds and energizes the nations that are behind, then the gratitude-flower of those particular nations will blossom inside the strong nation's heart, and the fragrance of the gratitude-flower in turn will strengthen and accelerate the strong nation's progress towards its destined goal. The fragrance of the flower will inspire it, and from this inspiration it will get abundant life, abundant light and an abundant sense of achievement and perfection.

3

The great mystic thinker Kahlil Gibran said something most soulfully true: "The significance of man is not in his attainment but in what he longs to attain." The past has not given us what we really need. Granted, the past was something significant, but right now it pales into insignificance when we measure it against our dream: not against what we are, but against what we want to become. What we are now is a semi-animal, but what we want to become is a full, complete and total God. The present-day world has achieved quite a few significant things. It has acquired money-power, technology-power, machine-power, but unfortunately it has not acquired soul-power. It has acquired the power to destroy humanity, but this has not brought it any satisfaction. It longs for peace, harmony and unity.

Dream and reality are two different things. Right now reality is most deplorable, and man's dream is a far cry. The reality that the United Nations can offer to the world at large is not quite satisfactory. But for that we cannot blame the United Nations. For that we must blame each individual person in each and every country. Unless each human being cooperates most soulfully with the will of the United Nations, reality will remain a series of painful accidents, and dream will remain a chimerical castle in the air. Unless and until each country becomes inseparably one with the ideals of the United Nations, we can never be happy and fulfilled.

Millions of people know about the United Nations and admire its capacities, its willingness, its eagerness, its good will. But how many people are ready to become one with the very soul of the United Nations? Millions of people can meet together, but if there is no soul's bond, no soul's unity, then all nations will prove to be veritable beggars. In the matter of inner strength, inner power and real achievement, thousands of minds, thousands of bodies, thousands of vital beings or emotional feelings can join together, but if the soul's bond is not established, there will always be loneliness, separateness and dissatisfaction. The soul of the United Nations has to be accepted by all nations, and only then will a sense of completeness, perfection and satisfaction be attained.

Each individual should feel that he belongs not to his own nation, but to all nations. That does not mean that he will neglect his own nation and devote all his attention to other nations. Each human being who has the energy and willingness to be of service to other nations will also have the willingness to serve his own country soulfully and unselfishly. While serving his own country, he has to feel that it is becoming one with other nations. He has to feel that his own arms are becoming one with his eyes. His arms are his power of work and his eyes are his power of vision. His vision takes him throughout the length and breadth of the world, whereas his arms remain where he himself is. With his vision he sees the needs of his brothers and sisters of the world. Then with his arms he can work to fulfill those needs. But he can do this only when he feels that he has gone far beyond his little family and has accepted the world-family as his very own.

The greatest wise man of the past, Socrates, taught us something very profound when he said, "I am not an Athenian, nor am I a Greek. I am a citizen of the world." If each individual in each nation can proclaim this message, if each individual in each nation can consciously and devotedly feel that he does not belong to a little family called "I and mine" but to a larger family called "we and ours," then the message of the United Nations, the message of brotherhood, of peace, of soulful sharing, can easily be received, embraced and embodied by all the peoples and all the nations of the world.

The Garland of Nation-Souls

A garland is the embodiment of God's Smile and man's achievement. God's divine Smile is supremely expansive, and man's divine achievement is eternally impressive. Now, where is the garland of nation-souls? It is inside the boat of the United Nations.

When a nation's outer life listens to the inner dictates of its soul, its earthly desires decrease, its Heavenly aspirations increase, its human wants are lessened and its divine needs are heightened. It envisions the Truth transcendental and grows into God's Pride supreme. The great philosopher Arthur Schopenhauer once remarked, "Every nation ridicules other nations, and all are right." Fortunately, all nations, with no exception, will one day be flooded with God's perfect Perfection, at God's choice Hour. The nations that are aspiring consciously are hastening God's Hour. The nations that are aspiring unconsciously are inwardly valuing God's Hour, and soon their aspiration will increase. The nations that are wallowing in darkness are God's so-called failures, but before long even they will open their eyes and, along with their forerunners, will hear God ringing the bell of inner victory.

The ascending aspiration of the fully awakened souls and the descending Blessing-Light of God can eventually transform the face of the entire globe.

Imperfection and impossibility we cherished yesterday. Today, imperfection and impossibility are our unwanted guests. Tomorrow, they will be seen nowhere. Perfection and divinity will be our most welcome guests.

The nation that soulfully cries for inner development and devotedly cries for outer growth can alone be in the vanguard of nations.

Why does a nation fail? A nation fails because it does not want the sustaining Truth to be on its side. When does a nation fall? A nation falls when it deliberately and vehemently resists the idea of being on the side of Truth. How can a nation succeed? A nation can succeed by following the Truth within and without. The very pursuit of Truth can make a nation free, meaningful, purposeful and fruitful. How can a nation flourish? A nation can flourish by seeing no difference between the Creator and the creation. A nation can flourish by loving the world not for what the world will give in return, but for the sake of love itself. Real love, selfless love, never ends, never fails. Love is its own immediate reward.

To me, the real worth of the United Nations lies in the united principles of its members. It is in these united principles that one can see the fruit of true inner oneness and divine perfection. The united principles of this great world-body must needs have cooperation from each and every member. If there is no cooperation, then even the very best principles will bear no fruit whatsoever. The present-day world needs cooperation.

Supremely significant are the words of former Secretary-General U Thant: "I can think of no worthier task for a man or a woman to be engaged in than that of creating the tools for international cooperation and working for the betterment of his fellow human beings." Also, he soulfully affirmed: "Our work at the United Nations gives us the privilege of contributing actively from day to day in the ardent process of building peace."

Each nation has a soul of its own. The soul is at once God's illumining activity and the nation's fulfilling capacity. Each nation is the involution of its highest light and the evolution of its inmost power. Immortality is the homeland of the soul. Eternity is the life of the soul. Infinity is the reality of the soul. With deepest joy we see here at the United Nations the promising hearts of 200 nations. Each nation is unique, for in and through each nation the Lord Supreme wants to fulfill Himself. Each nation is chosen by the Supreme, to fulfill Him in an unprecedented, unique manner.

Each nation has five members in its family: inspiration, aspiration, realization, revelation and manifestation. The body needs inspiration. The vital needs aspiration. The mind needs realization. The heart needs revelation. The soul needs manifestation.

The body wants to walk. The vital wants to run. The mind wants to fly. The heart wants to dive. The soul wants to become.

Inspiration without aspiration cannot see God. Aspiration without realization cannot reach God. Realization without revelation cannot glorify God. Revelation without manifestation cannot fulfill God.

Each nation right now needs peace. Man seeks peace because he needs peace desperately. Man welcomes peace because it is in peace alone that he can have his own true achievement and fulfillment. The moment he needs peace, he has to feel that sooner or later he will receive it. And when his inner being is flooded with peace, he has to spread this peace. Man spreads peace because he knows that he has to conquer or transcend death.

War and peace. In his outer being and inner being, each man has two familiar words: war and peace. Outer war we all know well. Inner war is constant. At every moment a sincere seeker has to fight against his own doubts, imperfections, limitations, bondage and death. When we achieve victory in the inner world, only then can we claim to be worthy children of God, true representatives of God. At that moment God beckons us to Him, to use us in His own Way.

Man invents war. Man discovers peace. Man invents war from without. Man discovers peace from within. The smile of war is the flood of human blood. The smile of peace is love, love divine, below, above. The animal in man wants war—war to devour the sleeping, snoring world. The divine in man needs peace—peace to feed the hungry world.

What Is the United Nations
Really Doing for Humanity?

What is the United Nations really doing for humanity? This is a most challenging question. Each person is competent to answer this lofty question according to his soul's light. First, I wish to tell you what the United Nations is, according to my own inner light.

> The United Nations is humanity's colossal hope.
> The United Nations is Divinity's lofty promise.
> Hope needs assurance from Heaven's soul.
> Promise needs receptivity from earth's heart.

Let us take the United Nations as a human being. Naturally, this human being has a body, a vital, a mind, a heart and a soul. The body of the United Nations is trying to serve humanity. The vital of the United Nations is striving to energize humanity. The mind of the United Nations is longing to inspire humanity. The heart of the United Nations is crying to love humanity. Finally, the soul of the United Nations is flying to embrace humanity.

The United Nations as a whole wants to offer peace. Peace and the United Nations are inseparable. What is peace? Peace is a very complicated word when we live in the physical world or in the mental world. In the physical world, we see children quarreling and fighting all the time. They derive satisfaction from fighting. This satisfaction is their peace. In the mental world, people are always doubting, suspecting, arguing and doing quite a few things that the spiritual world may not appreciate. Nevertheless, the mental world gets satisfaction from using its intellectual capacities, its doubt-weapons.

Doubt and suspicion themselves are the peace of the unillumined mental world. But there is also an inner world. In the inner world is self-giving, and self-giving is immediately followed by love-becoming, truth-becoming and perfection-becoming.

Peace does not mean the absence of war. Outwardly two countries may not wage war, but if they inwardly treasure aggressive thoughts, hostile thoughts, that is as good as war. Peace means the presence of harmony, love, satisfaction and oneness. Peace means a flood of love in the world family. Peace means the unity of the universal heart and the oneness of the universal soul.

To me, the United Nations is great. Why? Because it has high principles. To me, the United Nations is good. Why? Because it leaves no stone unturned to transform these principles into living realities. To me, the United Nations is divine. Why? Because it is the fond child of the Supreme dedicated to promoting world peace.

The world may notice a yawning gulf between the principles of the United Nations and the realities of the world. But the world must remember that in the transformation of principles into realities, time is a great factor. The world is old, and it has old ideas, old idiosyncrasies, old propensities. The United Nations is young, very young. Nevertheless, if we go deep within, we can easily observe how many things have been accomplished in the brief years of the United Nations existence. For the first 13 years of our human life, we consciously or unconsciously wallowed in the pleasures of ignorance without even thinking of trying to live a better life, a higher life, a more perfect life. In order to go from thinking about these goals to actually achieving them, we need a great length of time.

We expect everything from the United Nations, but we forget that it is still a child, and the child has to grow. If we nourish the child, encourage the child and appreciate him for what he already has offered, only then will the progress of the child be satisfactory. If we place a very heavy load on the child's shoulders while he is still small and weak, whose fault is it if he cannot carry it? It is our fault. The child may think that he can carry the entire world on his shoulders, but the parents know that the child's wish will be fulfilled and manifested only in the course of time.

Unfortunately, the world is a bad parent. The world's pressures are attacking the United Nations, but the world's appreciation is rarely seen or heard. The way the United Nations has become a victim to the world's criticism is most deplorable. The world knows how to criticize, but the world does not know how to become one with the soul of the United Nations and see how hard its light is trying to come to the fore, to establish peace and light on earth. The United Nations is trying to ameliorate the teeming afflictions that sit so heavily on the world's shoulders. It is trying hard to cancel the world's inequalities.

The United Nations sings one song: the song that says it is love-power that will conquer the world. No other power can conquer the world. From this song we realize something more: when love-power conquers, the conquest is not for the expansion of influence, but for the illumination of existence.

The United Nations is the meeting place for the big brothers and the small brothers of the world. The big brothers are at times reluctant to share with the small brothers their capacities, their wisdom and their achievements. The little brothers at times want to grab the capacities, wisdom-light and achievements of the big brothers without working for them. When the younger brother sees that his older brother has his master's degree, he too wants to get a master's degree. His wishful thinking far transcends his reality's capacity. But if the big brother offers a little bit of light from his abundant light to the little brother, the little brother feels that he has gained world-knowledge all at once.

The big brother wants only one thing: satisfaction. The little brother also wants only one thing: satisfaction. Complete satisfaction dawns only when the elder brother and the younger brother smile simultaneously. If I smile because of my achievement, and you cannot smile because of your lack of achievement, I will have no real satisfaction. The smiles must be reciprocal, universal. The need of the younger brother and the abundant capacity of the older brother can be amalgamated. When they are united, both can smile together.

The younger brother wants nothing but acceptance; the older brother wants nothing but self-transcendence. Acceptance and self-transcendence are the prerequisites of action and perfection. Action means acceptance of the world, no matter how weak or insufficient it is, for its present and future transformation. Perfection means constant transcendence of today's achievement by means of self-giving. Self-giving is immediately followed by self-transcendence, and in self-transcendence alone do we get the message of perfection.

People say the United Nations is imperfect. I wish to ask them what organization on earth is perfect? They say the United Nations has not fulfilled human needs. I say we have not given full opportunity, not to speak of full authority, to the United Nations to do the needful. Imperfection is the fate of human organizations until divinity reigns supreme within them. There is no organization which is totally perfect. But there are organizations which, knowing perfectly well that they are imperfect, still pretend to be perfect. There are also human beings who know perfectly well that they are imperfect, but do not want to lift one finger to achieve perfection. Again, there are organizations and human beings that cry for perfection and work for perfection, for they know it is only perfection that can bring satisfaction. Without the least possible hesitation we can say that the heart of the United Nations is crying for perfection. In the inner world, the entire being of the United Nations is crying for perfection. But perfection is not a one-man game. It is a collective game that is played by all men. The capacities of all human beings have to be offered, as well as the capacities of all those who work for the United Nations.

Many years ago, Woodrow Wilson and others had a lofty, sublime, supernal vision: a world united and at peace. The

United Nations is trying to transform that vision into reality. Let us consider the fulfilled vision as the height of Mount Everest, while the present reality is the foot of Mount Everest. We are now still at the foot of the mountain, but if we go deep within, we will see that we have definitely begun to climb. We know how difficult it is to climb all the way to the top, but slowly and steadily the soul of the United Nations is offering its light to the body of the United Nations, which is the world, so that it can reach the height of the lofty vision seen so many years ago. This vision cannot and will not always remain a vision, because inside the vision itself is reality. We may see the manifestation of that reality in 400 years, in 100 years, in 50 years or in ten years, depending on what the world sees and feels in the heart of the United Nations on the strength of its identification. This identification can be achieved only if we live in the soul.

Peace, freedom, progress, perfection—these are the four rungs of the cosmic ladder which the United Nations has perfectly housed in the unseen recesses of its heart. Peace we achieve when we do not expect anything from the world, but only give, give and give unconditionally what we have and what we are. Freedom we achieve only when we live in the soul's light. If we live in the light of the soul, if we can swim in the light of the soul's sea, immediately we grow into and achieve the true inner freedom. Progress we achieve by our self-expansion. How do we expand ourselves? We expand ourselves only by offering our inner concern, which comes directly from the very depths of our heart. Perfection we achieve only when we see the One in the many and the many in the One. When we see the One in the many, we have to feel that sound-reality is nourishing the entire cosmos. Silence-reality is the soul and sound-reality is the body of the United Nations. From the body of the United Nations we receive the message of union. From the soul of the United Nations we receive the message of perfection.

If we want to know what the United Nations is really doing for humanity, each one of us has to ask himself or herself a few questions, for each of us represents humanity. Are we really seeing the bright side of the United Nations? Are we sincerely working for the fulfillment of the vision of the United Nations? Are we wholeheartedly trying to become one with the struggles of the United Nations? Are we deeply concerned about the United Nations and its role in the world community? If we can answer all these questions in the affirmative, then the soul of the United Nations is bound to reveal to us what it has already done for mankind, what it is doing for mankind and what it will be doing for mankind. What has it done? It has brought down the message of promise from the Highest in Heaven. What is it doing? It is proclaiming this promise to the length and breadth of the world. What will it be doing? It will be manifesting this promise not only in and through the seekers of Truth, Light and Perfection, but also in those who deliberately deny the potentialities, the capacities and the soul-realities of the United Nations.

The United Nations has a big heart. Irrespective of human attainment, irrespective of human assessment, it will offer its nectar-drink to each human being on earth. Its soul's offering will be felt first in the soul's world, the inner world. Then it will be seen in the outer world. Finally, it will be accepted wholeheartedly by the entire world. In its acceptance of this undeniable truth-reality, humanity will move one step higher on the ladder of divine manifestation and earthly perfection.

The United Nations as an Instrument of Human Unification

What is an instrument? An instrument is the manifestation of the Creator's Dream. The United Nations is an instrument, a significant instrument, an unprecedented instrument of God for His searching, aspiring and loving humanity. This instrument is the joy of the Creator and, at the same time, the joy of the creation. The United Nations embodies both Heaven's Vision and earth's reality. There was a time when Heaven's Vision was only partially manifested as reality. We called it the League of Nations. Then the League of Nations was transformed into reality, and it became the United Nations.

We are all in the process of evolution. Once upon a time we were in the animal kingdom; now we are in the human world, consciously trying to transcend our earth-bound realities. While we were in the animal kingdom, the message of unification did not exist. There was only the message of destruction. In the human world, the message of unification is something real and significant. Nevertheless, unification is still a far cry.

Unification and perfection go together. They complement and fulfill each other. Unification and satisfaction go together. They complement and fulfill each other. Unification is the song of the many for the One. Perfection is the song of the One for the many. Satisfaction is the song of the One in the many and the many in the One.

When we think of the United Nations, the first thing that comes to our mind is reliance. Self-reliance is good; inter-reliance is better. Union in multiplicity and multiplicity in union is by far the best. There is a great difference between self-reliance and independence. When we rely on ourselves, on our inner being, our own divinity acts in and through us. At that time, we are relying on the Inner Pilot, who is in all and who is our All. But when we advocate independence, our uncontrolled, undisciplined, rebellious and autocratic nature comes to the fore. Independence we experienced in the animal world. When we exercised our independence, what did we do? We quarreled, we fought, we attacked and we destroyed one another. The message of unification can never breathe in this type of independence. The forest of independence is full of conflicts and contests that nobody actually wins. In the garden of self-reliance, the soul's light comes forward from within us to show us the way and the goal.

The United Nations is not merely an organization to be appreciated, admired or adored. Rather, it is the way, the way of oneness, that leads us to the supreme Oneness. It is like a river flowing towards the source, the ultimate Source. The United Nations wants to lead the world to the destined Goal, where oneness-light and oneness-delight reign supreme.

In this world we see that some people just talk, some talk and then act, others talk and act simultaneously, while still others only act and let others talk for them. Finally, there is a type of person who just acts for the sake of divine action. This is the supreme category. Without the least possible hesitation, I would like to say that the United Nations belongs to this category. I do not know about the United Nations outer achievements. But being a seeker of the highest Truth who lives in the inner world, who sees and feels and knows what the United Nations is doing, I am perfectly familiar with the inner achievements of the United Nations.

The United Nations is a real mother, and the world is like a child in front of it. You may say that the world is so vast, whereas the United Nations is just a small building. But you have to know who is playing what role on earth. The United Nations is playing the role of the mother. The mother offers her very existence to feed and nourish the child and give the child the message of Light, the message of Truth, the message of Reality. The child very often ignores the mother's offering or takes it for granted. Sometimes the child accepts the mother's wisdom, but when it is a matter of offering gratitude to the mother, the child consciously or unconsciously forgets.

When a mother does everything for her child, it is not news. But if the child offers a glass of water to his mother, then that is news. It is not unusual for a mother to work like a slave for 24 hours a day to please her child, but when the child does something most insignificant for his mother, the world takes note of it. The United Nations receives help from the four corners of the globe—financial help, all kinds of help—and that becomes news in the world. But what the United Nations at every second is offering or trying to offer inwardly and outwardly is not news; this the world does not recognize.

The world is blind; it needs God-Vision. The United Nations has God-Vision in abundant measure. The world is weak; it needs soul-power. The United Nations has soul-power in abundant measure. The world is suffering; it needs heart-consolation. The United Nations has heart-consolation in abundant measure.

With utmost love and humility, the seeker in me tells the world to talk less and listen more. Listen to whom? To the United Nations. The United Nations has much to offer in every field. It unmistakably has the soul-peace and the heart-dedication to be the first and foremost instrument of human unification.

God the Creator is at once the Silence-Seed and the Sound-Tree. As the Silence-Seed, as the Silence of the transcendental Height, He embodies His own highest Height and deepest Depth. As the Sound-Tree, He offers to His creation His own achievements. Silence prepares; sound reveals. Sound offers what silence is. Silence tells us who God is, and sound tells us where God is. Who is God? God is man's eternal cry for the highest transcendental Supreme. Where is God? God is in man's soulful smile. Where a sincere and soulful smile looms large in our existence, we see God's very real Presence. Silence-life is embodied in the soul of the United Nations. Sound-life is embodied in the body of the United Nations.

The outer reality is not always the true reality. The outer reality sometimes, if not always, deceives us. The outer reality very often comes to us in the form of temptation, whereas the inner reality always comes to us in the form of emancipation, liberation and salvation. If we go from the outer reality to the inner reality to challenge and fight against it, then we are acting like a fool. The inner reality will never surrender to the outer reality. But if we become one with the inner reality, which is our silence-life, which is God's Vision, then we can bring it to the fore and transform the outer reality. The outer reality is the reality created by the human mind, the mind which is still imperfect in many ways. This very mind will one day be transformed, perfected, divinized and immortalized. By whom? By the Inner Pilot and by the divine forces of the inner world.

Critics are of the opinion that the United Nations is sometimes not brave enough or quick enough. It is very easy to criticize an organization. But an organization is composed of human beings, and human beings are still far, far from perfection. Therefore, how can we expect a human organization to be perfect? It is the human in us that criticizes, not the divine in us. The divine in us sees the perfection in ourselves and in others. A real seeker feels that he is growing from perfection to greater perfection to infinite Perfection; from light to more light to abundant, infinite and immortal Light. The achievements of the United Nations in the outer world are the achievements of an organization that is still growing towards perfection. Eventually a day will come when it will be totally perfect, and that day will come when you and I and all those who work in the United Nations become totally perfect.

There are many ways to serve the United Nations: with the physical body, the physical mind, the inner heart and the soul's good will. I wish to say that all the services rendered by each individual are necessary, for through them all we offer our limited perfection to the soul of the United Nations. Each individual not only has the message of perfection, but actually is the message of perfection. If we can offer this message of perfection to the soul of the United Nations, then the capacity of the United Nations will multiply itself infinitely.

Let us not ask the United Nations what it has done. Let us not even ask ourselves what we have done. Let us only ask ourselves whether we are of the United Nations and for the United Nations. If we say we are of the United Nations, then our source is peace, infinite peace. And if we say we are for the United Nations, then our manifestation is delight, eternal delight. Our source is peace and our manifestation is bliss on earth. If we know what we are and what we stand for, then the United Nations can become for us the answer to world-suffering, world-disharmony and world-ignorance.

The inner vision of the United Nations is a gift supreme. This vision the world can deny for 20, 30, even 100 years. But a day will dawn when the vision of the United Nations will save the world. And when the reality of the United Nations starts bearing fruit, then the breath of Immortality will be a living reality on earth.

God's Compassion and
the United Nations Dedication

Unlimited and unconditional is God's Compassion. Thoughtful and fruitful is the dedication of the United Nations. God's Compassion is ignored by humanity. The dedication of the United Nations is quite often misunderstood and at times suspected by humanity. Why does this happen? It happens precisely because ignorance still lords it over us. God's Compassion is inner protection unseen. God's Protection is illumination visible everywhere. Dedication is the soul's promise to God and to mankind. This promise the soul made to humanity and to Divinity perhaps hundreds or thousands of years ago. The promise the soul has made to humanity and to Divinity must be fulfilled.

The promise the soul has made to humanity is very simple: it will kindle the flame of aspiration in the heart of humanity. It will make the earth-consciousness a perfect instrument so that it can receive God's Light from Above in infinite measure. It will make the heart of earth feel Heaven's Light, Heaven's Delight and Heaven's Existence. Finally, it will make of earth the divine clarion-voice of Heaven.

The soul has made a promise to Divinity that it will manifest God the Absolute, God the Omniscient, God the Omnipotent and God the Omnipresent on earth. The soul has promised God that with the help of the physical, the vital and the mind, in short, with the help of the entire being, it will manifest Him here on earth. Here on earth the soul will offer the perfection of dedication to God.

Dedication is delight, the delight of the heart. When we dedicate ourselves to something, our very dedication expands our consciousness, and we begin to feel our inseparable oneness with that thing. When we dedicate ourselves to God, we feel that our oneness with God is something real and fulfilling. Then each time we dedicate something of ours, we expand our love for God. Our very reality, our earth-bound reality, is then transformed into a Heavenward journey.

Dedication to the highest Self is conscious union. It is in union that life becomes meaningful and fruitful. A life without the feeling of union is confusion and frustration. Today's dedication is bound to be transformed into tomorrow's perfection. When perfection dawns, we can foresee clearly all our divine wishes, we can feed all our divine aspirations and finally, we can fulfill all our divine needs. The human dedication of the United Nations has the key to open God's Palace. God's Compassion shows man where his infinite treasure lies within himself.

A child of God was blessed with a vision. This child was President Woodrow Wilson. He had the vision of a League of Nations. That League of Nations was a tiny plant. Now the plant has grown into a huge banyan tree: the United Nations.

Needless to say, the world is still not perfect. Since the world is not perfect, world-opinion cannot be perfect. Since we are imperfect, we consciously or unconsciously, willingly or unwillingly, indulge in criticism. We see conflict in our thoughts, ideas, plans, ideals and missions. There are many on earth who find fault with the ideals and the dedicated service of the United Nations. But from the spiritual point of view, I wish to say that each action and each dedicated service is not a mere experiment of man; it is an experience of God in and through the United Nations. Each individual nation may, for its own reasons, want to be united with other nations. But the United Nations means the union of the various ideas, thoughts and feelings of all the individual nations and, therefore, the expansion of oneness.

In the United Nations, unity can be achieved through manifested multiplicity. This is what we see and feel in the heart of the United Nations. We have been seeing the desire for supremacy in man since the dawn of civilization. Each human being wants to be a bit stronger than the rest; each human being wants to surpass the rest. But from the spiritual point of view, we can surpass others only when we embrace the ideal of oneness. One nation can surpass other nations only by becoming one with them in their suffering, in their joy and in their achievements. When we become one with others, we surpass not only the capacity of our own achievements and of their achievements, but also the capacity of limitation itself. Real supremacy comes when we grow into vastness. If we become vastness itself, then who or what can be superior to us?

It is not in vain or without any purpose that the United Nations has come into existence. God's Vision has to be manifested here on earth. The suffering nations need a place for consolation; the sacrificing nations need a place for appreciation. From the spiritual point of view, the United Nations is struggling and striving for something meaningful and fruitful. What it needs, it has: both human dedication and divine Compassion. The Compassion of God has been unceasingly descending upon the United Nations. Now it is up to the world. But the sleeping, unaspiring, unawakened world is not yet receiving the light of the United Nations. There are many things the world could receive from the dedication of the United Nations; but if the world is not receptive, it is not the fault of the United Nations. God is all Compassion, He is all-giving; but if we don't want to receive His Light the way He wants to offer it, that is not His fault.

The heart of the United Nations is dedication. The soul of the United Nations is concern. The body of the United Nations is for the illumining expansion of human consciousness.

We sow the seed; the seed germinates. First we see a tiny plant; then we see a huge tree. When we go deep within, we see that a seed was sown here in the earth-consciousness, and that seed had boundless potentiality. God's Light is here for humanity to receive on a practical level, in an earthly manner. God's Light is here to illumine us. Consciously and unconsciously the world is receiving this Light from the United Nations; but the United Nations is not being recognized, and this fact is deplorable. The human beings who have become the instruments to offer the light that the soul of the United Nations has, may not be fully aware of what they are doing. When they see imperfections in others, when they see their own limited capacity, at times they feel frustrated. But the divine in each delegate, in each representative from each individual nation and in each staff member is all wisdom. It has chosen the right instrument to offer something worthwhile to both God and humanity: the United Nations.

Here people meet, not for mere consolation when the world is in conflict, not for mere justification, not for mere glorification, but for the feeling of universal oneness and for the manifestation of God's Perfection on earth in a practical manner. At the United Nations we see the oneness of mental philosophy and psychic religion. All philosophies and all religions are running towards the same Goal. Philosophy teaches us how to see the Truth, and religion helps us in applying the Truth in our outer life. Here at the United Nations all major religions meet. Here the outer wealth of desire and the inner wealth of aspiration meet, each one offering its might. From the spiritual point of view, in the soul's region, the contribution of each nation is sublime.

The United Nations is the chosen instrument of God. To be a chosen instrument of God means to be a divine messenger carrying the banner of God's inner Vision and outer manifestation. One day the world will not only treasure and cherish the soul of the United Nations, but also claim the soul of the United Nations as its very own with enormous pride, for this soul is all-loving, all-nourishing and all-fulfilling.

A Spiritual Goal for the United Nations: Is It Practical?

A spiritual goal for the United Nations: is it practical? Without the least possible hesitation I venture to say that it is highly practical. It is not only practical, but also practicable. Something more: it is inevitable. But what is the spiritual goal for the United Nations? Its goal is to become ultimately the savior of the world's imperfection, the liberator of the world's destruction and the fulfiller of the world's aspiration.

My heart tells me that the United Nations has a divine ideal. My soul tells me that this ideal is going to be transformed into the supreme Reality. Soulful concern is the essence of the United Nations ideal. Fruitful patience is the substance of the United Nations ideal. Supernal fulfillment will be the essence of the United Nations reality. Sempiternal perfection will be the substance of the United Nations reality. What is reality? Reality is the inseparable oneness of Infinity's Smile and Eternity's Cry.

The great philosopher Aristotle once aptly remarked, "Some men are just as firmly convinced of what they think as others are of what they know." The firm conviction of the United Nations is both the confident flight of sublime thought and the glowing depth of knowledge-light.

Today's United Nations sees the nations as true friends. Tomorrow's United Nations will see the nations as real sisters and brothers. Today's United Nations offers hopeful and soulful advice to mankind. Tomorrow's United Nations will offer fruitful and fulfilling peace to mankind. Today's United Nations feels truth, light and delight in its loving heart. Tomorrow's United Nations will manifest truth, light and delight with its all-embracing soul.

My aspiring heart has a soulful message to offer to all the nations that have formed the garland of nation-souls which is the United Nations. The message is this: There are two stumbling blocks on the path to human unity. They are doubt and insecurity—doubt in the mind and insecurity in the heart. There are also two stepping-stones in this path. They are faith and surrender—faith in oneself and conscious surrender to God's divine Will.

True, we have lost and misused thousands of golden opportunities, but we cannot lose or exhaust God's infinite Compassion. Out of His infinite Compassion, He will ultimately make us feel and realize the transcendental Truth. However, this can be done in two ways. One way is to realize the highest Truth at God's choice Hour; the other way is to realize the Truth when we feel the time is ready, according to our own sweet will. When we open our eyes at God's Hour, we fulfill God in His own Way. When we open our eyes at our own selected hour, we fulfill God in our own way. The desire in us fulfills God in its own way. The aspiration in us fulfills God in God's Way. Needless to say, our aspiration is bound to manifest the ultimate, absolute Reality on earth sooner. In the manifestation of absolute Reality on earth, the face of earth will be transformed into the face of Heaven.

The spiritual message that the soul of the United Nations offers to the world at large is for Eternity. Its message is this: Today's imperfect and unfulfilled man is tomorrow's absolutely fulfilled and supremely manifested God.

The Inner Message of the United Nations

The outer message of the United Nations is peace.
The inner message of the United Nations is love.
The inmost message of the United Nations is oneness.
Peace we feel. Love we become. Oneness we manifest.

The United Nations has a mind, a heart and a soul. Its mind tries to offer the message of flowing peace. Its heart tries to offer the message of glowing love. Its soul tries to offer the message of fulfilling oneness. In the near future, a day will dawn when the inner message of the United Nations will be absorbing to the child, elevating to the common man, thought-provoking to the highly educated and inspiring to the seeker.

Each delegate is a force; each representative is a force; each nation is a force. The origin of this force is a particular will. This will can be either the divine Will or the human will. The human will wants to work with the world and in the world only on one condition: that it will be able to gain supremacy over others and maintain this supremacy. The divine Will wants to work in the world, with the world and for the world without expecting anything from the world. The human will, at most, tolerates the world. The divine Will constantly wants to liberate and fulfill the world. The human will wants to control and lead the world. The divine Will wants to transform, glorify and immortalize the world. The human will in us needs the soul's expanding and illumining purity. The divine Will in us wants the Goal's blossoming divinity.

The League of Nations was a dream-seed.
The United Nations is a reality-plant.
The aspiring and serving life of man's universal oneness
   will be the Eternity-Tree.

The goal of the United Nations lies not simply in thinking together, but in thinking alike. Each individual has every right to love his nation. But he must also dedicate himself to improving his nation's relationships, inner and outer, with the rest of mankind, so that all can run together towards the universal good of humanity. In the words of Pope John XXIII: "It is our earnest wish that the United Nations organization may become ever more equal to the magnitude and nobility of its tasks, and that the day may come when every human being will find therein an effective safeguard for the rights which derive directly from his dignity as a person, and which are therefore universal, inviolable and inalienable rights."

All nations together can build a temple.
All nations together can make a shrine.
All nations together can worship a Deity.
At the entrance of the temple, the divine protection
   shall smile.
Upon the shrine in the temple, the supreme illumina-
   tion shall smile.
Within the heart of the Deity, the absolute Perfection
   shall smile.

Here at the United Nations an inner voyage has begun. In its inner voyage, the United Nations has to brave many difficulties and setbacks. As we all know, defeats and failures are mere stepping-stones in our onward march to perfection. At the end of its voyage, there is every possibility that the United Nations will be the last word in human perfection. Then the United Nations can easily bloom in excellence and stand at the pinnacle of divine enlightenment.

The Soul-Love of the United Nations

The soul-love of the United Nations is life-examination, life-improvement and life-perfection.

Life-examination makes our deeds on earth meaningful.

Life-improvement makes our rest in Heaven blissful.

Life-perfection makes our dream in Heaven and on earth fruitful.

The soul-love of the United Nations has the fragrance of Divinity's rose on the physical plane and the benediction of Immortality's bird on the spiritual plane.

Mind-love, heart-love and soul-love. Mind-love is just an opinion. Heart-love is a firm conviction. Soul-love is an everlasting illumination. Opinions at times confuse us. Convictions at times disappoint us. But illumination always makes us see the height of Truth and the Feet of God. It also makes us see that it has silenced the roaring lion of darkness in the outer world, and that it has fed the soaring bird of light in the inner world.

The soul-love of the United Nations teaches us three most important things: patience, expansion and oneness. Patience is not peace. But patience eventually shows us the way to peace, world peace. Expansion is not an act of self-aggrandizement. But expansion can easily be a life-offering and love-building reality. Oneness does not indicate a lack of opportunity for revealing and manifesting individual uniqueness. Oneness is like the beauty and fragrance of a lotus. They do not prevent each petal of the lotus from revealing and manifesting its own uniqueness.

The soul-love of the United Nations has a philosophy of its own. It says that each nation has its own significant truth. One nation will not and cannot overthrow the realization and revelation of another nation. Instead, the realization and revelation of one nation can easily complement the realization and revelation of another nation.

The soul-love of the United Nations has a religion of its own. This religion is a silently unified wisdom. In this silently unified wisdom a supremely unifying life looms large.

What is the soul? As the great philosopher Voltaire pointed out, "Four thousand volumes of metaphysics cannot teach us what the soul is." It is the soul alone that can teach us, through our own inner experience, what the soul is. But before the soul teaches us about itself, we have to unlearn the teachings of the obscure, uncertain and doubting mind and, at the same time, we have to learn the teachings of the loving, uniting and illumining heart.

In order to know the soul-love of the United Nations, we have to choose to be free, and we have to be free to choose. When we are within the confines of history, we have to choose to be free. When we are in the sky of evolving spirituality, we have to be free to choose. Soul-love is free will. Soul-love is free choice. When a nation's free will chooses self-giving, its free choice expedites God-becoming. In self-giving and God-becoming is the confluence of the outer luster of the United Nations and the inner effulgence of the United Nations. This confluence will, without fail, be a glorious vision for both mortals and immortals.

From the spiritual point of view, the soul-love of the United Nations will always remain resourceful in all problematical situations, untiring in the discharge of its national and international duties, sagacious in its pursuit of inner knowledge and inner wealth, and spontaneous in its willingness to add to the peace, love and joy of searching and ascending humanity; for the soul is the child of both Infinity's Dream and Eternity's Reality.

The Heart-Peace of the United Nations

The heart says to peace, "Peace, I need you."
Peace says to the heart, "Heart, I need you."
Without peace, the heart is fruitless.
Without the heart, peace is homeless.

The inner heart of the United Nations is flooded with peace.
The outer heart of the United Nations is trying to spread
peace all over the world.
The outer existence of the United Nations is a colossal
hope.
The inner existence of the United Nations is a fulfilling
reality.

The heart of the United Nations has peace.
The mind of the United Nations seeks peace.
The vital of the United Nations needs peace.
The body of the United Nations is for peace.

The presence of peace in the heart is divine oneness.
The presence of peace in the mind is divine illumination.
The presence of peace in the vital is divine dynamism.
The presence of peace in the body is divine satisfaction.

The goal of the United Nations is world-peace.
The secret of the United Nations is self-sacrifice.

There are two types of people: one wants peace, the other
does not. Many nations have joined together to form the outer
body of the United Nations. Peace is expected from each of
these nations. But if any nation tries to surpass other nations

ruthlessly, then that particular nation will never be claimed as its own by God's Pride, Heaven's Delight and earth's gratitude. When all nations work together devotedly and untiringly, only then can they embody universal oneness and reveal universal love.

The General Assembly

The General Assembly is a gathering of a very special family. Unlike most families, this family knows what to say, what to do and what to become. It knows how to love, how to serve and how to fulfill.

What to say? The members of this family say that they wish to live together forever. What to do? They try to understand one another; they try to share with one another their inspiring ideas and glowing ideals. What to become? They try to become a cry; they try to become a hope; they try to become a promise; they try to become a smile—a cry that elevates them, a hope that feeds them, a promise that reveals them, a smile that immortalizes them. How to love? They try to love with their illumining souls. How to serve? They try to serve with their searching minds and their striving vitals. How to fulfill? They try to fulfill by steering God's Dream-Boat towards the Golden Shore.

The General Assembly signifies interdependence. It represents a song of the community of nations, a song of aspiring souls. While singing this song, these souls will climb high, higher, highest until they one day reach the transcendental Vision of world union. While singing this song, these souls will march far, farther, farthest until they one day reach the transcendental Reality of universal peace.

There is also another reason why this time of year is most significant. Thirteen years ago tomorrow, one of the great pilots of the United Nations passed behind the curtain of Eternity: Dag Hammarskjöld died in a plane crash. But before his soul flew to the highest realm of consciousness, it left behind the quintessence of its love for humanity, its wish for peace throughout humanity and its feeling of oneness with humanity. Dag Hammarskjöld was a man of God and a servant of humanity. The body and soul of the United Nations treasure the quintessence of his love of truth, light, peace and universal oneness.

Here we are all seekers. We, too, belong to a family, a spiritual family. We are all praying for world-peace, world-harmony and world-union in a divine and supreme way. Today the General Assembly begins once again with new hope, new determination and new aspiration to discover something more illumining and more fulfilling. We, too, the seekers of infinite Truth and Light, can begin again today with new hope, new determination and new aspiration as we try to become more spiritual, more sincere and more dedicated. In this way we can serve the Inner Pilot of the United Nations, the Inner Pilot of the entire world-family, in a most illumining and fulfilling way.

No Nation Is Unwanted

No nation is unwanted. Every nation is wanted. Every nation is needed. Every nation is indispensable. But each nation is great only if it has deep love for other nations and soulful self-giving to other nations.

Why does an individual love others? An individual loves others because he knows that if he does not love others, then he remains imperfect and incomplete. Why does an individual give of himself to others? An individual gives of himself to others because he has discovered the undeniable truth that self-giving is truth-loving and God-becoming. And what applies to an individual human being can equally, appropriately and convincingly apply to a nation.

Sir Winston Churchill once made a most significant remark: "When abroad, I do not criticize the government of our country, but I make up for it when I come home." Self-criticism is necessary; self-criticism is obligatory. If each nation values self-criticism when it is at home, then perfection-sun will not remain a far cry. Self-criticism is the harbinger of self-enquiry. Self-enquiry is the harbinger of God-discovery. In God-discovery man rises above the ignorance of millennia.

A nation may have hundreds of good, divine and even astonishing qualities, but if that nation is wanting in one important inner quality, the feeling of oneness, then it cannot have true satisfaction. Everlasting satisfaction is out of the question. Again, if a nation is not blessed with many striking qualities and illumining capacities, but nonetheless has the all-important sense of inseparable oneness, then that nation is the creator of fulfilling joy, the owner of fulfilling joy and the distributor of fulfilling joy.

Each nation is a petal of a flower. If one petal is ruined, the entire flower loses its perfect beauty; and when a flower loses its beauty, it loses its most important quality. Each nation is like a note in a song. If one note is not properly sung, the entire song is ruined.

Each nation has the capacity to fulfill all nations through self-giving, and this self-giving is nothing other than God-becoming. Here at the United Nations, each nation can offer its illumining capacities and fulfilling qualities to all the other nations. Together all nations will walk, together all nations will run, together all nations will fly and dive towards the same goal, the goal of everlasting Truth. When we reach and become the everlasting Truth, we shall see that we have transformed the animal in us and immortalized the divine in us.

How can a nation be happy, purposeful and fulfilled? A nation can be happy, purposeful and fulfilled if it thinks less and meditates more. A nation can be happy, purposeful and fulfilled if it plans less and acts more. Thinking is quite often confusing. Planning is quite often frustrating. Too much thinking and too much doubting and suspecting go together. Too much planning and too much worrying and indecision go together.

Meditation and action have a different story to tell. Illumining meditation is self-discovery. Illumining action is self-mastery. The more one can meditate soulfully, the sooner one reaches the destination. The more one can act devotedly, the sooner one manifests God-life, truth-love and light-delight. A seeker-nation with God-Life sees God's Body, the universe. A seeker-nation with truth-love feels God's Heart, the universal Reality. A seeker-nation with light-delight becomes God's Soul, the universal Goal.

Each Nation Is Great

A nation is a limb of the universal body. Each limb is necessary, essential and indispensable. Each nation represents humanity's hope, humanity's promise and humanity's progress manifested in a unique way.

Hope was our yesterday's treasure. Promise is our today's treasure. Progress shall be our tomorrow's treasure.

Each nation can be great by virtue of a few divine qualities. A nation can be great by virtue of its simplicity. A nation can be great by virtue of its sincerity. A nation can be great by virtue of its humility. A nation can be great by virtue of its sense of duty, both national and international. A nation can be great by virtue of its prosperity, both inner and outer. Finally, a nation can be great by virtue of its generosity, constant and supreme.

A great nation is that nation which offers inspiration to other nations. A greater nation is that nation which offers concern for other nations. The greatest nation is that nation which offers its heart's spontaneous love to other nations.

With inspiration we begin to form our universal family. With concern we strengthen our universal family. With love we feed and fulfill our universal family.

The divine greatness of a nation lies in its self-offering today. The divine greatness of a nation lies in its God-becoming tomorrow. The divine greatness of a nation lies in its God-revelation today. The divine greatness of a nation lies in its God-manifestation tomorrow.

Each individual nation can be a perfect example of self-offering, God-becoming, God-revelation and God-manifestation. How? If a nation lives in the heart, then self-offering is not only possible, but also inevitable. If a nation lives in the soul, then God-becoming is not only possible, but also inevitable. If a nation tries and cries for the transformation of the whole universal family of nations, then God-revelation can no longer remain a far cry. God-revelation then is not only possible, but also practicable and inevitable. Finally, if a nation cares sincerely, devotedly, soulfully and unconditionally for the perfect perfection not only of its own existence, but also of the entire universe, then God-manifestation is bound to take place.

In size, in capacity, in receptivity, all nations may not have the same status. But each nation is indispensable in its own way. Each nation is like a drop, a tiny drop or a mighty drop, in the vast ocean of divine, fulfilling, fruitful consciousness. It is all the drops combined that make up the ocean. Again, it is the ocean that manifests or fulfills its existence through the different drops, small and large alike.

Each nation is humanity's conscious cry for perfect Perfection. It is in and through each nation that humanity can make the ultimate progress. This ultimate progress is spiritual brotherhood, divine Reality, immortal Life in the life of the mortal, and infinite achievement in the heart of the finite.

A Living Shrine

Those who work and serve at the United Nations are the most fortunate people on earth, for God has chosen us to be His instruments to serve Him in mankind. Please try to feel that the United Nations is not a mere building, but a place of worship, a place where all human beings can worship and pray to God. This place is a living shrine for the Supreme.

If we do not do what we are expected to do now, if we do not offer our soulful meditation and soulful dedication now, in days to come we shall feel sorry that we missed a true divine opportunity. But if we do the right thing now, in the near or distant future the Supreme will entrust us with still higher tasks. Each time we do something for Him, He is pleased with us and gives us the opportunity to do something higher and more fulfilling in His cosmic Game.

God is pleased with us if we try every day, every hour of our inner and outer existence at the United Nations to be soulful and self-giving. If we are soulful and self-giving, then our Goal can never remain a far cry. On the contrary, instead of seeing ourselves running alone towards the Goal, we shall see that our Goal is also running towards us.

Peace: The United Nations Soulful Promise

Sri Chinmoy gave the following talk in Sydney, Australia, on March 6, 1976.

I happen to be a seeker at the United Nations. My sole aim there is to serve the body and soul of the United Nations in silence with my prayer and meditation. I do not know anything about politics, but I do know about oneness with the Highest. In the United Nations there is a group of genuine seekers who come together two times a week to serve the United Nations with their soulful prayer and meditation. We feel that this inner prayer and meditation can and will help in boundless measure to bring peace, light and bliss to the world. It takes time, but we see that it also takes time for the United Nations to achieve its goals.

Right now, the achievements of the United Nations are far from satisfactory. But we feel that still there is hope. The United Nations is a symbol of man's inner cry, inner oneness. Outwardly, the members of the United Nations do make mistakes. But even if we make mistakes, that does not mean that we shall never arrive at our goal. No, mistakes are merely rungs in the ladder of our inner progress. If we have an inner urge to do the right thing, to grow into the right thing, to fulfill the divine within us, then there comes a time when we do become perfect instruments of God. So we cannot judge the United Nations on its present achievements. We cannot judge the United Nations by what it has already offered us. We can only judge the United Nations on its soulful promise, its promise that it will one day flood the world with boundless peace.

God has countless children and countless divine qualities, but I wish to say that His fondest child is peace. This world of ours has everything save and except one thing, and that is peace.

What is peace? Peace is satisfaction. Each individual has his own way of discovering peace or defining peace. A child breaks something or makes a clamorous noise, and that gives him satisfaction and makes him feel peace for a few seconds. Similarly, the destructive vital of a particular nation may come to the fore and conquer or destroy another nation. The victorious nation gets joy; it feels satisfaction and peace for a brief period of time.

Each individual and each nation has a way of defining peace, appreciating peace and achieving peace. But most of the time this peace is false peace; it is peace that is inevitably followed by frustration. A child breaks something; then a few minutes later he wants to break something else. One thing is not enough; he wants to break ten things. Constantly his hunger to break things is increasing. A nation conquers another nation, but it is not satisfied. The nation wants to conquer a few more nations. In this way there is no end to its hunger. Frustration follows achievement and abiding peace is never found.

Julius Caesar said, *Veni, vidi, vici:* "I came, I saw, I conquered." He conquered, but inside him was nothing but a barren desert. By conquering we cannot have happiness. If he had said, "I came, I saw, I became one with you," then he would have had real peace. Real peace comes only if we say, "I have come to serve you, I am becoming part and parcel of your existence-reality." Then we will feel perfect peace.

Right now fear, doubt, conflict, tension and disharmony are reigning supreme. But there shall come a time when this world of ours will be flooded with peace. Who is going to bring about this radical change? It will be you—you and your brothers and sisters. You and your oneness-heart will spread peace throughout the length and breadth of the world. Peace is unity. Peace is oneness, within and without.

Dag Hammarskjöld: The Mind's Brilliance and the Heart's Oneness

This is our soulful tribute to the immortal memory of the U.N. Pilot, Dag Hammarskjöld. According to human wisdom, death is a halt, where all movements cease for good. But according to divine wisdom, death is a step we all take while walking along Eternity's Road. We wish to offer our soulful homage to the great soul, Dag Hammarskjöld, and also to invoke this great soul to bless us in our life of inner aspiration and our life of outer dedication.

When we think of Secretary-General Dag Hammarskjöld, we come to realize that in him the age-long battle between the mind and the heart had come to an end. In him, the mind and the heart had become good, intimate friends. We all know that when there are two friends, both friends walk together towards the same destination. But in his case, we observe something extraordinary. Although the mind went along the road of illumination and the heart marched along the road of liberation, they were in perfect harmony with one another, in perfect understanding. We think that if two persons are true friends, then they must walk together. But this is not necessary. If there are two goals that eventually merge into one goal, then these subordinate goals can be reached separately before we reach the ultimate Goal. Illumination was the first goal, which Dag Hammarskjöld's mind wanted to attain. Liberation of the aspiring heart was the second goal, which his heart wanted to achieve. So his mind went to the illumination-shore and his heart went to the liberation-shore. Then from the illumination-shore and the liberation-shore, the mind and the heart together went to the Perfection-shore. The Perfection-shore is the ultimate Goal of each human being.

Dag Hammarskjöld was a great man, a good heart, a dedicated life, a possessor of soulful vision-light. Something more: he became a fulfilling bridge between humanity's excruciating pangs and Divinity's illumining Compassion.

Usually the mind's brilliance and the heart's oneness do not and cannot go together, because the mind tends to enjoy a sense of separativity. But Dag Hammarskjöld's life amply proved that the mind's brilliance and the heart's oneness can and do go together.

Usually the selfless purity of the body and the bold dynamism of the vital do not run abreast. Again, Dag Hammarskjöld was a rare exception.

Usually there is a yawning gulf between earth's practical reality-body and Heaven's theoretical vision-soul. But it is unmistakably true that Dag Hammarskjöld bridged that yawning gulf in his life's short span.

The practical man in Dag Hammarskjöld teaches us: "Do not look back, and do not dream about the future, either. Your duty, your reward, your destiny are here and now." The theoretical soul in Dag Hammarskjöld shares with us:

The moon was caught in the branches:
Bound by its vow,
My heart was heavy.
Naked against the night
The trees slept. "Nevertheless,
Not as I will . . ."
The burden remained mine:
They could not hear my call,
And all was silence.

A great man is, indeed, a great power. Human power cleverly avoids justification. Divine power does not avoid justification, for there is no need on its part to do so. It knows that justification is only another name for its selfsame reality. The Secretary-General's wisdom-light reveals to us, "Only he deserves power who every day justifies it."

We desire many things. Sometimes we do not know what we desire or why we desire. Unlike us, God knows what He wishes for us: independence. The seeker in Dag Hammarskjöld not only tells us about God's Wish for us, but also tells us when we can attain it: "God desires our independence—which we attain when, ceasing to strive for it ourselves, we 'fall' back into God."

Dag Hammarskjöld was a man of unparalleled responsibility. Responsibility demands capacity, which he had in abundant measure. Out of his heart's magnanimity, he shares with us the quintessence of responsibility and capacity: "Somebody placed the shuttle in your hand: Somebody who had already arranged the threads."

The seeker's life is not necessarily a bed of roses. Sometimes it can seem to be a bed of thorns. When the seeker Dag Hammarskjöld's inner crisis loomed large, his frustration-life voiced forth: "What I ask for is absurd—that life shall have a meaning. What I strive for is impossible—that my life shall acquire a meaning."

Again, when the same seeker's life-tree blossomed into a glorious satisfaction, he immediately and unreservedly expressed his joy:

"That chapter is closed. Nothing binds me.
Beauty, goodness,
In the wonders here and now
Become suddenly real."

The sterling simplicity of Secretary-General Dag Hammarskjöld's life illumines our life of aspiration, and his soul's ever-glowing luminosity fulfills our life of dedication. A flying earth-plane killed his body, only to help his soul fly to reach the highest height. His Heaven-bound soul got the immediate opportunity to see the Face of the Beloved Supreme.

Dag Hammarskjöld was a seeker in the purest sense of the term. He was a seeker of the highest order. His heart cried for the satisfaction of mankind. His mind cried for the illumination of mankind. His body is no longer on earth, and yet his soul is not only in Heaven, but also on earth. His soul-bird flies from Heaven to earth, from earth to Heaven. When it comes to earth, it comes with new hope, new light, new illumination, new compassion and new consolation. Then it becomes one with us, and when it flies to Heaven, it carries our inner cry, inner thirst and inner hunger. It also carries our insufficiencies, our weaknesses, our misunderstanding, our lack of sympathy and oneness. It carries to Heaven all the darkness of the unlit, strangling world that we live in or have created for ourselves. Each time the soul of this great seeker, Dag Hammarskjöld, comes down, it brings down for us at the United Nations and for seekers all over the world the hope that awakens mankind, the consolation that sustains mankind and the compassion that eventually lifts up humanity's fate to the golden heights of tomorrow's dawn.

All quoted excerpts from Markings *by Dag Hammarskjöld.*

U Thant: A Chosen Instrument of God

U Thant was a chosen instrument of God. U Thant was a chosen instrument of man. God gave him His Compassion-Sky to offer to man. Man gave him his suffering-sea to offer to God.

U Thant started his earthly sojourn as a Rangoon, Burma Buddha-son. The Absolute Supreme gradually made him into a universal wisdom-son and a universal blessing-gift.

To most people, peace is something that belongs to the dream-land. Since it belongs to the dream-land, we only talk about it. To U Thant, peace was something that belonged to the reality-world. Therefore, he lived in the reality-world of peace and was a solid and treasured member of the reality-peace-world.

To us, oneness is something that we think we want but do not actually feel the need for. To U Thant, oneness was something of constant need, something indispensable. His heart cried for this oneness and the Lord Supreme, the Author of all good, fulfilled his heart's burning desire.

The United Nations gave U Thant the opportunity to speak to the world-body as a supreme leader of mankind. In return, U Thant gave the United Nations the message of world-mind-illumination, of world-heart-perfection and of world-life-satisfaction.

U Thant was the supreme choice of the United Nations, and God was pleased with him. But God wanted U Thant to please Him still more. Therefore, he made U Thant a pioneer voice of light from the higher worlds.

Simplicity, purity and integrity he was. He was a child's simplicity. He was a saint's purity. He was a God-lover's integrity.

He struggled calmly; he suffered ceaselessly; he hoped sleeplessly. Again, he knew how to dream of success, and he knew how to become the river of progress.

We feel that man is bad, imperfect and undivine. U Thant's conviction was that man is good, perfect and divine, for that is what each individual in the inner world eternally is.

U Thant's life of humility was the result of his heart's nobility. His heart's nobility was the result of his soul's unparalleled divinity.

Sincerity spoke through him, integrity breathed in him, spirituality walked with him. He knew the outer world-problem: ignorance. He knew the inner world-answer: meditation. And this he practiced in silence.

God practiced His Silence-Meditation in and through U Thant. God practiced His Sound-Dedication in and through U Thant.

U Thant was at once God-humility and man-dignity. He was at once man-frustration and God-illumination. He was at once the soulful son of God and the faithful slave of man.

Self-demonstration he ruthlessly shunned. Self-transformation he practiced. God-perfection he sought to embrace and treasure. Before him, the United Nations was great, divinely great. With him, the United Nations became supremely good.

In the inner world he was God's Promise, God's Promise to the outer world. In the outer world he was man's confidence, man's confidence in becoming a dedicated instrument of the inner world.

Earth gave him responsibility. Heaven knew it and saw it. Heaven gave him authority but, unfortunately, earth did not know it or did not care to know it. His heart of brotherhood was misunderstood. His life of sacrifice was not valued. But his vision of a oneness-goal will eternally be pursued by aspiring humanity.

An Asian seed he was. A world-flower he became and forever and forever he shall remain.

They Say and We Say

They say that the United Nations is a mere dream. We say that it is a dream that can grow into reality. Dream is the seed-essence. Reality is the fruit-substance.

They say that the United Nations is not independent. We say that there is no need for the United Nations to be independent, for the United Nations lives in the illumining heart of humanity and for the aspiring life of humanity.

They say that the United Nations is not powerful. We say that unless the world has given the United Nations the opportunity to show all its strength, both outer and inner, but especially inner, how can it say that the United Nations is not powerful? The world knows what outer strength is. But what is inner strength? Inner strength is divine revolution. The possessor of inner strength revolts against disappointment-bondage. He revolts against ignorance-night. He revolts against imperfection-mortality.

They say that the United Nations is not stable, that it is constantly changing its policies. We say that if a new policy embodies more light, more perfection and more satisfaction, then naturally it is the bounden duty of the United Nations to adopt the new policy instead of unwisely clinging to the old policy.

They say that the United Nations is losing its moral authority. We say that if this is true, then the world is losing its sanity very rapidly, and heading towards an explosion of a devastating character.

The United Nations Needs
Self-Giving Servers

The United Nations needs completely self-sacrificing and self-giving servers. May God, our Lord Supreme, shower at every moment His choicest Blessings upon the devoted heads and dedicated lives here at the United Nations, so that their most significant contributions towards the perfection of the United Nations can be felt convincingly and unmistakably by the lovers of the United Nations all over the world.

The United Nations has a beautiful, more beautiful, most beautiful soul. Through their own souls, may the self-giving servers bring to the fore the most perfect brilliance of the United Nations, to illumine the unlit ignorance of the human mind and fulfill the aspiring human life, which longs for oneness in peace and peace in oneness throughout the length and breadth of the world. May the self-giving servers expedite the unprecedented journey of the United Nations, which is undoubtedly the journey of the oneness-heart and not the journey of the division-mind.

The United Nations is not a man-made building. It is God's own transcendental Dream, which He is now translating into His universal Reality. What we need is an illumined mind, a heart of love and a life of sacrifice. Once we have achieved these divine qualities, we shall see that the United Nations is the only answer to the world-problems and offers the only way to bring joy, perfection and satisfaction to humanity's life on earth.

World-oneness can be felt and manifested only when the entire world sincerely looks to the United Nations for guidance. He who says that the United Nations has failed is utterly mistaken. He who believes that the United Nations is a fruitless hope is also completely mistaken. But he who thinks and feels that the United Nations embodies God's Oneness-Dream and Promise, which at God's choice Hour will blossom into His universal Reality, is absolutely right.

God's Dream and God's Promise can never, never remain unfulfilled and unmanifested. Those who have failed and those who are going to fail as instruments of God's Dream and God's Promise will eventually leave the United Nations. Those who are absolutely for the United Nations and only for the United Nations will survive and prevail to manifest and fulfill God's Oneness-Dream.

The United Nations has not failed and will never fail. Only the human mind has failed. Now the heart has to come to the fore and declared, "All human beings are my sisters and my brothers. I can be happy only if I make my sisters and brothers also happy. If I stay one step ahead of them, they will not be happy. If I have a true heart of oneness, I will not want to go ahead of them. Although right now I may have a little more capacity than they have, I have to shower my brothers and sisters with affection." It is the heart's affection that will solve our problems, not the mind's superiority.

Let us say that you are richer and more capable than I am. If you are offering your capacities to me and helping me bring my own capacities to the fore, I will appreciate, admire and love you. But if you constantly try to keep yourself above me, I will not love you. If you really want my love, you will try to bring me to the level where you are.

Right now the world-powers want to get satisfaction only by staying one step ahead of everyone else. This is not the right approach. They are trying to win the admiration and love of others through force, which is absurd. True admiration and love will come only when there is oneness. God the Creator is superior to us; He is our Lord Transcendental. But He does not lord it over us. No! He has become one with us. Just because the Infinite is ready to become one with the finite, the finite is able to love and worship the Infinite.

The world will love the poor because they are suffering. It will not love the great powers if they criticize the United Nations and threaten not to support it. God has created the world, and He who has created the world will take care of the world. Therefore, the United Nations should not feel threatened. If the United Nations does not get help from the great powers, the self-giving servers of the United Nations will go to every door and say, "Use your heart, use your heart!" Finally the hearts of the great powers will compel them to help. But even if their hearts remain closed, the United Nations will get help from the poorest countries. The poor countries will not have reluctance, unwillingness or contempt. If they give only one cent with love, the self-giving servers of the United Nations will adore them because of their oneness-heart.

United Nations Day

What does United Nations Day signify? It signifies a day of universal hope, a day of universal promise, a day of universal peace and universal oneness. Hope brightens humanity's present deplorable fate. Promise encourages humanity's speed, which embodies success and progress. Peace enlightens humanity's age-old ignorance. Satisfaction, which is founded upon oneness, the oneness that we long for in our world family, will one day dawn in our aspiring heart and our dedicated life.

The United Nations is not a mere building. It is not a mere concept. It is not wishful thinking or even a dream. It is a reality which is growing, glowing and manifesting its radiance here, there, all-where, throughout the length and breadth of the world. All those who are sincerely crying for a oneness-family are receiving light according to their receptivity from the soul of the United Nations.

Hope

Hope is my mind's secret fear.
Hope is my heart's sacred courage.
Hope is my life's daring experience.
Hope is my soul's illumining success
And my soul's fulfilling progress.
Hope is my Lord's ascending Perfection
And my Lord's transcending Satisfaction.

We, the members of the Meditation Group at the United Nations, have only one friend—a soulful friend, a oneness-friend—and that friend is hope. We started our journey with our hope-friend. Hope-friend and hope-life were synonymous in our case. This hope-life was firmly established on February 29th, 1972, when we had the golden opportunity to meet with former Secretary-General U Thant, who embodied colossal hope for the entire world.

U Thant's life itself became the glorious flowering of hope. A simple schoolteacher from Burma became the principal teacher of the comity of nations. Here his teaching did not come to an end. He went one step ahead to serve divinity in humanity with the message of the all-illumining and all-fulfilling Truth, the Truth that has no alternative. The message of his soulful heart was: "No compromise, no compromise with falsehood! Truth is paramount. Truth alone can save, illumine, perfect and fulfill the world."

Hope-vision he discovered. Hope-realization he became. Hope-illumination he offered to the world at large. This was our beloved brother, U Thant, the U.N. Pilot who will ever be remembered for his simplicity-life, kindness-heart and oneness-soul. In him we observe that the finite hope of today does not have to remain finite and fleeting forever. It can slowly, steadily and unerringly grow into infinite, life-saving and life-illumining Reality.

U Thant's compassion was at times misunderstood by human souls. But his oneness with all nations big and small, his oneness with all and sundry, was never, never misunderstood. What he was, what he is and what he will remain forever is simplicity's oneness, purity's oneness and divinity's oneness.

The Inner Role
of the United Nations—I

The U.S. State Department invited Sri Chinmoy to come to Washington on June 6, 1980 to address its Open Forum, a policy discussion group inaugurated during the Vietnam War to acquaint policy-makers with different points of view on critical issues of the day. Sri Chinmoy was asked to speak on the inner role of the United Nations. Sri Chinmoy also delivered this same talk at United Nations headquarters on June 13, 1980 as part of his Dag Hammarskjöld lecture series.

When I speak of the United Nations, my mind, heart and soul immediately compel me to speak of the United States in the same breath. When I speak for the United Nations, my mind, heart and soul are immediately blessed by the prosperous and generous soul of the host state—the Empire State, New York.

The term united has always had a special appeal to all human souls, and this transcendent idea has remained prominent down the sweep of centuries. There was a time when America was under the repressive yoke of Great Britain. Then America fought dauntlessly and sleeplessly for its rightful independence. At first, the newly liberated Americans and their beautiful, vast land were sadly wanting in oneness. But there came a time when a new dawn of oneness-glory broke upon the glowing and illumining horizon. Americans felt the supreme necessity of a united country, and the 13 colonies gradually, steadily, unerringly and selflessly became unified. Similarly, although at the present time peace is not reigning supreme in the United Nations, there shall definitely come a time when peace-flood will inundate the united nations around the globe.

Who could have envisaged that the 13 colonies would one day develop into such a powerful country—50 states standing indivisible, united by none other than the Hand of the Supreme Being? For the United States, the heart-throbbing and life-illumining credo "united" had its birthless and deathless origin in the hearts of the great Americans whose names are synonymous with the lofty principles of liberty, justice and oneness. The founder of the nation, George Washington; the vision-light, Thomas Jefferson; the wisdom-sun, Benjamin Franklin; and the tireless fighter, John Adams: these powerful luminaries, along with others, bravely dreamt of unity for the 13 colonies.

Again, it was a great son of the United States, Woodrow Wilson, who had the pioneer-vision of the League of Nations, the hallowed source of the United Nations. Some people are of the opinion that the League of Nations totally collapsed and failed, but I cannot see eye to eye with them. The League of Nations did not fail. We must view the League of Nations as the loving mother and the United Nations as her most promising child. When parents leave the earth-planet, their children often bring forth more aspiration-light, more vision-power and more manifestation-delight than the parents themselves were able to do. Unmistakably, it is from the dying parents that a bright new light comes to the fore. When the children successfully offer much more than their parents to the world at large, we never think that the parents were hopeless and useless in comparison. On the contrary, we perceive a most significant inner connection between them, a link founded upon inner growth. We see that the children are marching and progressing in their parents' footsteps. For this reason we can safely say that Woodrow Wilson's League of Nations actually offered its wisdom-light to its future child, the United Nations.

The United States and the United Nations are divinely destined to run abreast. Not in vain is the headquarters of the United Nations in the United States and in New York, the capital of the world. This dynamic and fascinating world capital draws the world's attention at every moment. Is there any place that can be more appropriate than New York City to house the vision of universal oneness, which is in the process of being realized and manifested in the heart and soul of humanity?

True, at times the United States and the United Nations are not on the best of terms. But each knows perfectly well that the one adds tremendous value to the other in terms of prestige, recognition, self-awareness and oneness-perfection. Inwardly they know that they truly need and deserve each other. In silence, unreservedly the United States gives the United Nations confidence-light. In silence, unreservedly the United Nations gives the United States oneness-height. Being a seeker, in my silence-heart I feel that the concept of the United Nations has verily come from the United States, unconsciously if not consciously, for the United States had this united feeling two hundred years ago, whereas the United Nations is only a few decades old.

The inner role of the United Nations amuses the intelligentsia, inspires the world-peace-lovers and nourishes the world-oneness-servers. God has showered His choicest Blessings upon the inner role of the United Nations. When we contemplate the idea of a "role," we immediately think of either responsibility or challenge. But when it is a matter of the inner role, there is no such thing as responsibility or challenge; there is only one self-giving Divinity, which is breathlessly growing into a self-becoming Reality.

The United Nations is often misunderstood. Perhaps its fate will always remain the same. But is there anybody who is not misunderstood, including God? Misunderstanding is the order of the day. That does not and cannot prevent the United Nations from making its soulful self-offering through the creation of a oneness-home for all.

The United Nations has been marching resolutely and triumphantly towards its inner goal. Indeed, the remarkable leadership of its Secretaries-General has made its outer success and inner progress not only convincing, but also fulfilling. Our present Secretary-General, Kurt Waldheim, throws considerable light on the inner role of the world organization:

We are not faced with many separate problems, but with different aspects of a single over-all problem: the survival and prosperity of all men and women, and their harmonious development, physical as well as spiritual, in peace with each other and with nature. This is the solution we must seek. It is within our power to find it.

Secretary-General Waldheim's predecessor—the Supreme Pilot of the United Nations, U Thant—valued unreservedly the inner or spiritual obligations of the United Nations.

I have certain priorities in regard to virtues and human values . . . . I would attach greater importance to moral qualities or moral virtues over intellectual qualities or intellectual virtues—moral qualities, like love, compassion, understanding, tolerance, the philosophy of live and let live, the ability to understand the other man's point of view, which is the key to all great religions . . . . And above all, I would attach the greatest importance to spiritual values, spiritual qualities.

Secretary-General Dag Hammarskjöld offered the hallowed message-light that each individual has a responsibility to his own inner role. According to him, each individual must strive inwardly as well as outwardly to achieve abiding peace:

Our work for peace must begin within the private world of each one of us. To build for man a world without fear, we must be without fear. To build a world of justice, we must be just. And how can we fight for liberty if we are not free in our own minds?

Illumining leaders from all over the world who are serving the United Nations remind us of the undeniable fact that the earth cannot exist without the world body—the United Nations—in spite of its apparent failings and problems.

Secretary-General Trygve Lie's precious message ran:

> The one common undertaking and universal instru-
> ment of the great majority of the human race is the
> United Nations. A patient, constructive, long-term use
> of its potentialities can bring a real and secure peace to
> the world.

The outer role of the United Nations is greatness remarkable. The inner role of the United Nations is goodness
admirable. The supreme role of the United Nations is fullness
adorable.

Greatness our mind desperately needs. Goodness our heart
sleeplessly needs. Fullness our life breathlessly needs.

Greatness surprises the curious world. Goodness inspires
the aspiring world. Fullness fulfills the serving world.

Greatness is blessed with an outer challenge. Goodness is
blessed with an inner promise. Fullness is blessed with an
integral perfection. Challenge awakens, promise expedites
and perfection immortalizes our varied capacities.

Greatness is sound-amplification. Goodness is silence-
enlightenment. Fullness is God-satisfaction.

The pillars of the United States, its Presidents, call upon us
to dedicate ourselves to the most significant cause that the
United Nations embodies. Needless to say, the world organi-
zation is God's gracious experiment and precious experience.
Such being the case, we must feel an inner obligation to par-
ticipate in this aspect of God's cosmic Drama. The late
President John F. Kennedy spoke not only to his fellow
Americans but to all his fellow beings when he proclaimed:

> My fellow inhabitants of this planet, let us take our
> stand here in this assembly of nations. And let us see if
> we, in our own time, can move the world towards a just
> and lasting peace.

President Carter has also powerfully encouraged his country

to remain part and parcel of the United Nations. He tells us that real leadership and continuous service to mankind are inseparable:

> There is no possible means of isolating ourselves from the rest of the world, so we must provide leadership. But this leadership need not depend on our inherent military force, or economic power, or political persuasion. It should derive from the fact that we try to be right and honest and truthful and decent.

The favorite son of New York, Senator Daniel Moynihan, former United States Ambassador to the United Nations, expresses his country's sincere awareness of the sublime necessity of the United Nations:

> While there have been some calls to boycott the General Assembly, or not to vote in it, there have been but few calls for withdrawal from the United Nations. It is almost as if American opinion now acknowledged that there was no escaping involvement in the emergent world society.

The United States' Special Ambassador to the United Nations Law of the Sea Conference, Elliot Richardson—a heart of peace and a life of light—encourages, strengthens and spreads a global viewpoint:

> The interdependence of the world is an increasingly visible fact, and I believe that out of that fact is bound to emerge in due course a compelling—and comparably inspiring—concept of the opportunities for global cooperation.

A staunch supporter of the United Nations—indeed, the donor of the land upon which the U.N. stands—Nelson Rockefeller vividly draws the parallel between the roots of the

United States and the roots of the United Nations:

> The federal idea, which our Founding Fathers applied in
> their historic act of political creation in the eighteenth
> century, can be applied in this twentieth century in the
> larger context of the world of free nations—if we will
> but match our forefathers in courage and vision. The
> first historic instance secured freedom and order to this
> new nation. The second can decisively serve to guard
> freedom and to promote order in a free world.

As the Declaration of Independence of the United States is
an unparalleled discovery, so is the Charter of the United
Nations. The U.S. Declaration of Independence and the U.N.
Charter are humanity's two aspiration-dedication-realities. The
beacon-light of the Declaration of Independence shows countless human souls the way to their destined Goal:

> We hold these truths to be self-evident: that all men are
> created equal, that they are endowed by their Creator
> with certain inalienable rights, that among these are
> life, liberty and the pursuit of happiness, that to secure
> these rights, Governments are instituted among men,
> deriving their just powers from the consent of the
> governed.

The United Nations Charter bravely and heroically pro-
claims these rights for all of humanity and seeks:

> To reaffirm faith in fundamental human rights, in the
> dignity and worth of the human person, in the equal
> rights of men and women and of nations large and
> small, and to establish conditions under which justice
> and respect for the obligations arising from treaties and
> other sources of international law can be maintained,
> and to promote social progress and better standards of
> life in larger freedom.

Concern for and satisfaction in the towering achievements of the United Nations may be a confidence-voyage into the unknown, but never into the unknowable. The great messenger of the Catholic world, Pope Paul VI, during his visit to the United Nations in 1964, eloquently expressed the inner role of the United Nations:

> The Church considers the United Nations to be the fruit of a civilization to which the Catholic religion . . . gave the vital principles. It considers it an instrument of brotherhood between nations which the Holy See has always desired and promoted . . . . The convergence of so many peoples, of so many races, so many States, in a single organization intended to avert the evils of war and to favor the good things of peace, is a fact which the Holy See considers as corresponding to its concept of humanity and included within the area of its spiritual mission to the world.

When Pope John Paul II visited the United Nations in October 1979 and spoke to the General Assembly, Secretary-General Waldheim introduced him thus: "Your presence among us on this historic occasion is particularly encouraging since it dramatically reaffirms the great spiritual values which you represent and which inspire the Charter."

Pope John Paul II indeed reaffirmed the value of the inner United Nations and the spiritual dimension of world politics when he told the General Assembly:

> An analysis of the history of mankind, especially at its present stage, shows how important is the duty of revealing more fully the range of the goods that are linked with the spiritual dimension of human existence. It shows how important this task is for building peace and how serious is any threat to human rights.

The composer of the immortal "Hymn to the United Nations," the late maestro Don Pablo Casals, reminds us that individuals and their countries undeniably need the United Nations. He gives an inspired call for us to selflessly play our parts in the inner and outer roles of the United Nations:

> Those who believe in the dignity of man should act at this time to bring about a deeper understanding among people and a sincere rapprochement between conflicting forces. The United Nations today represents the most important hope for peace. Let us give it all power to act for our benefit. And let us fervently pray that the near future will disperse the clouds that darken our days now.

The outer role of the United Nations is a colossal hope. The inner role of the United Nations is a generous assurance. The supreme role of the United Nations is a prosperous satisfaction.

Hope is a growing plant. Assurance is a blossoming tree. Satisfaction is a delicious fruit.

At the present stage, the United Nations is a growing plant which is only 35 years old. Is it not absurd for us to expect the United Nations to solve overnight the overwhelming problems of centuries? Let the child-plant grow and glow, smile and cry. Then there shall come a time when this tiny plant will evolve into a huge tree, with countless leaves, sleepless flowers and spotless fruits—sheltering, inspiring and nourishing all those who desperately need its protection-shelter, rejuvenation-inspiration and satisfaction-nourishment.

The Inner Role of
the United Nations–II

Sri Chinmoy gave the following talk at the United Nations office in Geneva on June 16, 1980.

The inner role of the United Nations is a shadowless dream. The inner role of the United Nations is a relentless determination. The inner role of the United Nations is a breathless promise. The inner role of the United Nations is a sleepless struggle. The inner role of the United Nations is a faultless progress. The inner role of the United Nations is a deathless satisfaction. Prayer and meditation are of supreme importance if we are to manifest the inner role of the United Nations.

The inner role of the United Nations is a cry and a smile— an inner cry and an outer smile—and this inner cry and outer smile have to be perfected. The inner cry has to be genuine and the outer smile has to be soulful. The inner cry has to climb up to reach the highest pinnacle. The outer smile has to be illumined and fulfilled at the same time, and it has to reach the length and the breadth of the world.

The inner role of the United Nations is the link with the immortal power of infinite peace that spans the universe. This is the power that builds and does not break. This is the power of peace that inundates our inner beings and at the same time, our outer lives. This peace is also delight. It evolves slowly, steadily and unerringly towards the great and ultimate destination.

The inner role of the United Nations tells us that duty and responsibility have to be seen in a different light. Each member of the United Nations has a significant duty and responsibility. By virtue of our prayer and meditation, we have come to realize that duty is nothing other than opportunity, and that responsibility is another name for privilege. Therefore, to serve the unique capacity of the United Nations is to be blessed with a golden opportunity and a fruitful privilege.

The inner role of the United Nations tells us that success is fleeting, whereas progress is everlasting. It tells us that success on the physical plane, vital plane or mental plane cannot lead us to the final Goal; it is only progress that slowly and unmistakably leads us to our ultimate Goal. Again, when we reach the ultimate Goal, we get the message to go farther, for the ultimate Goal is not a fixed place; it is always in the process of transcending its own reality.

The inner role of the United Nations helps us discover a unique prayer, the prayer of prayers. At each moment, we have to pray not to conquer but to serve, and while serving, to free the oneness-reality in and around the world. We have to pray not to lead and again not merely to follow, but to become inseparably one with the comity of nations. Together, all the nations will dive the deepest, march the farthest and fly the highest.

Inner Flames at the
United Nations

Inner flames signify aspiration. Aspiration illumines the undivine in us and fulfills the divine in us. Our doubting mind is the undivine in us. Our loving heart is the divine in us. The doubting mind unconsciously and consciously tries to destroy the whole world. The loving heart consciously and unreservedly creates a new world: a world of hope, a world of light, a world of delight.

Aspiration is the inner cry. Both God and man have this inner cry. With His inner Cry, God claims us. With our inner cry, we follow God. God's inner Cry is for our perfection, and our inner cry is for God's Satisfaction.

We, the members of the Meditation Group at the United Nations, are all inner flames. We are trying, with utmost humility and sincerity, to be of service to each member of the United Nations, to the dream of the United Nations, to the pristine purity of the United Nations. Our capacity may be limited, but our willingness and eagerness to be of service to each member, to each ideal of the United Nations, is most sincere.

Here at the United Nations, all can be inner flames. No matter what an individual's post is, whether he holds the highest post or the lowest, he can undoubtedly be an inner flame, if his inner cry is genuine. Each conscious server of the United Nations, irrespective of his nationality or religious and cultural background, is undoubtedly an inner flame. And each flame serves the community of nations according to its capacity and according to its receptivity.

The original and pioneer flame was President Wilson. His dream of the League of Nations has blossomed into the United Nations. Once it was a tiny plant, but now it has grown into a huge banyan tree. The plant embodied the inner flame and now, as a huge banyan tree, it has countless flames.

God and Truth are one and inseparable. Truth and Light are also one and inseparable. Truth, when it starts manifesting itself, takes the form of Light, and this Light illumines and fulfills the seeker in us.

The seeker in us always wants to satisfy the little world and the big world. The world that we claim at the beginning of our life—our home, our parents, our brothers and sisters, our relatives—is the little world. But as our vision increases, as we look around and see a bigger world, an unhorizoned world awaiting us, at that time we claim the big world as our very own.

Each individual who has come to serve the United Nations represents his own country, his small world. But when he becomes part and parcel of the United Nations, the big world, at that time he is for all, for the entire humanity. He started his journey from his own country and then moved towards the goal of goals: universal oneness.

The United Nations wants to solve all the world-problems. It is more than eager to solve all the problems that the world could ever imagine. In various ways it is trying to solve the world's problems lovingly, devotedly, soulfully and unreservedly. A problem indicates ignorance, a problem indicates the dance of ego, a problem indicates human weakness. Each problem can be solved and will be solved by only one thing, and that is the message of union. This union comes to the fore only when we kindle the inner flame. We, as seekers, know perfectly well that it is the inner flames burning inside all the members of the United Nations that are inspiring the members to solve the problems of the world.

At the General Assembly each individual nation comes to offer its light, truth, willingness, capacity and sense of oneness. Each country embodies truth and light in its own way. But each country feels and knows in the inmost recesses of its heart that the light and truth it embodies cannot be sufficient. Therefore, it tries to accept and receive light from other countries. Similarly, each flame that each individual embodies cannot be sufficient to solve any world-problem or to illumine world-ignorance. What is needed is the unification of all the flames that are here, there and everywhere. All the flames that are here have to be collected so that they can muster their joint strength. At that time, the ignorance-dream that separates one country from another, one man from another, can no longer last. It will be replaced by wisdom-reality. And what is wisdom-reality? Wisdom-reality is the song of oneness. This song of oneness is founded only on self-giving, which is nothing short of truth-becoming. And truth-becoming is oneness with the all-embracing, all-loving, all-illumining and all-fulfilling Reality.

The higher reality is the soul in us; the lower reality is the body-consciousness. The lower reality aspires to grow into the higher reality. The higher reality inspires us to move forward in our quest for truth, light and peace. Most people think only of the lower reality of the United Nations—the body-reality, the U.N. building, where thousands of human beings are serving one cause. The actual building, the body-reality of the United Nations, immediately captures their minds. The outside world does not easily think of the soul-reality, which is the real reality of the United Nations. But it is the loving soul, the illumining soul of the United Nations that guides the body-reality, or try to guide it. The day will come when the outer world will realize that looming large inside the famous body-reality is the precious soul-reality.

We, the seekers and members of the Meditation Group at the United Nations are trying to serve both the soul-reality and the body-reality according to our limited capacity. Our capacity is limited, but our sincere efforts we place at the Feet of the Inner Pilot of the United Nations. This Inner Pilot is our fate-maker, the Author of all good, God.

The United Nations
and World-Union

The United Nations is the seed. World-union is the fruit. Both are of supreme importance. God-Vision embodies the seed. God-Reality reveals the fruit.

The United Nations is the morning. World union is the day. When the heart of the morning is flooded with inner light, divine light, the Light of God, then it is not only possible but almost certain that the entire day will be flooded with light. Only on very, very rare occasions do we see otherwise.

The United Nations tells us where truth is. World-union tells us what truth is. Where is truth? Truth is in self-giving. What is truth? Truth is man's transformation of his earth-bound nature.

The United Nations is a group of pilgrims on a journey. As the pilgrims walk along the path of light towards the same destination, they feel mutual appreciation. From appreciation they go one step ahead to love. Then from love they move to oneness. Oneness is the perfection of man in God and the satisfaction of God in man.

He who is a true member of the United Nations treasures a shared life in a shared world. A divided mind and a separated heart cannot quench the inner thirst of either the United Nations or the world. We must cultivate a new type of reality, a new type of truth. This truth is creative, illumining and fulfilling. This truth must awaken the dormant physical in us, marshal the unruly vital in us, illumine the doubtful and suspicious mind in us, and strengthen and immortalize the insecure heart in us. This truth is world-union.

Individuals must dive deep within and discover their pent-up reservoir of dynamic energy. This energy has to be released so that the human mind can enter into the universal

Mind, so that the human heart can enter into the eternal Heart and so that the human life can enter into the Life immortal.

Both the United Nations and the world have a special type of faith. This faith is evolutionary. It evolves from within to without, it evolves from unity to multiplicity and it evolves from multiplicity into the transcendental Reality.

The United Nations and world-union have an evolutionary faith and a revolutionary life. This revolutionary life wants to challenge the untold poverty and teeming ignorance of the world. The golden day is bound to dawn when this world of ours will be totally freed from poverty. But the outer poverty can be transformed only when the inner poverty is removed. Inner poverty is our lack of faith in our divine reality, our lack of faith in our capacity to realize the ultimate Truth. Unless and until we have put an end to our inner poverty, the problem of outer poverty cannot be solved.

Inner poverty is disharmony and restlessness; inner plenitude is peace, harmony and love. For the lover of the United Nations and world-union, the watchword must needs always be peace. Peace is found in self-giving and in our recognition of others' good and divine qualities. The more we see the divine qualities in others, the sooner we will establish world-peace.

Each nation has the strength and willpower of the Absolute. Each nation has the golden opportunity in the inner world to offer to the outer world a living hope and a living promise. This hope and this promise are not mental hallucinations or false aggrandizements of ego. They are an inner reality that the nation can easily bring to the fore. In the inner world all nations are equally important, for in the inner world each nation has a free access to world-peace, world-light, world-harmony and world-perfection. But in the outer life the nations that consciously aspire and cry for light are in a position to help the less advanced nations that are walking behind.

In the evolutionary process of human life, the first rung of the ladder is the United Nations, the second rung is world-union and the third rung is man's total and perfect Perfection.

If we do not place our foot on the first rung and then on the second, it will be simply impossible for us to climb up to the highest rung.

Each nation is a promise of God for God Himself. What we call world-union today has to be surpassed tomorrow by something else, and that something else is world-perfection. Union as such is not enough; the perfection of union is what we actually want. We may stay in a family even though we quarrel, fight and kill one another. Only if we can establish the sweetest feeling of oneness, does our union reach the acme of perfection.

2

Spiritual Awakening: Journey to Our Oneness-Heart

"It is with a feeling of deep respect for your life of selfless devotion and with appreciation of your good deeds that I want to extend my felicitations to you on the occasion of the 25th anniversary of your peace mission in the United Nations. . . . Your deeds are invaluable, for they cannot be measured by any economic or political parameters; they are noble and cure the human soul."

Mikhail Gorbachev
President of the Soviet Union
and Nobel Peace Laureate
Excerpt from a letter dated March 27, 1995
Shown during the U Thant Peace Award ceremony on Oct. 16, 1994

"I am so pleased with all the good work you are doing for world peace and for people in so many countries. May we continue to work together and to share together, all for the Glory of God and for the good of man."

Mother Teresa
Founder, Missionaries of Charity
and Nobel Peace Laureate
Shown receiving the U Thant Peace Award on October 1, 1994

Spirituality

Spirituality is truth-awareness.
Spirituality is life-emancipation.
Spirituality is oneness-manifestation.
Spirituality is perfection-satisfaction.

There are two types of spirituality. One is false, totally false. The other is true, absolutely true. False spirituality tells us that we have to negate and reject life and renounce everything in order to reach Heaven or in order to achieve peace, light and bliss in our human life. True spirituality tells us that we need not reject anything, we need not negate anything, we need not renounce anything. True spirituality tells us that we have to accept the world as it is, then transform both our inner world and our outer world for God-realization, God-revelation and God-manifestation. True spirituality tells us that it is only in God-realization, God-revelation and God-manifestation that we will find boundless peace, boundless light, boundless delight.

False spirituality is the dance of teeming desires. Desire is something that binds us to our possessions. There comes a time when we realize that although we are the possessor, we are actually slaves to our possessions. True spirituality is the song of aspiration. Aspiration liberates us from our binding and blinding possessions—material possessions, earthly possessions, possessions that do not help us to elevate our consciousness or reach our life's true inner and outer goals.

False spirituality is desire. The acme of desire is this: "I came, I saw, I conquered." Desire says, "I came into the world, I saw the world and I have conquered the world. Now I am in a position to lord it over the world." The strangling vital, the demanding vital, the authoritarian vital wants this world for its own enjoyment. But aspiration tells us something quite different. The teachings of aspiration are soulful, meaningful and fruitful. Aspiration tells us that individuals have come into the world to see, to love and to become one, to become fully aware of and inseparably one with their universal existence. Mere individual existence is of no avail. One has to have a free access to the universal life within.

Desire-life is the life of success; aspiration-life is the life of progress. The life of desire constantly demands, whereas the life of aspiration soulfully receives. The life of desire demands constantly from the world around us. The life of aspiration receives everything from the world within.

Success is short-lived satisfaction. Most of the time this short-lived satisfaction is followed by bitter dissatisfaction. In dissatisfaction, what actually looms large is frustration; and frustration is the harbinger of total destruction. Progress is our continuous, illumining and increasing satisfaction within and without. Those who follow the spiritual life know and feel the supreme necessity of progress. Every day, every hour, every minute, every second, a seeker has to feel that he is making progress. He is running fast, very fast, towards his destined Goal. He is climbing upward speedily, towards his transcendental Goal. He is diving deep within extremely fast, to reach the Absolute Lord in the inmost recesses of his heart.

In order to make progress, each seeker has to have two most reliable friends. Prayer and meditation are the two most intimate friends of a seeker of the absolute Truth. When the seeker prays to the Absolute Supreme, he feels his Lord's existence above, far above, his mental vision—let us say in Heaven. But when he meditates, he feels that his Lord Supreme is deep within his heart—in the inmost recesses of his loving, aspiring heart. His prayer tells him that his God is above. His meditation tells him that his God is within. When he reaches his Lord on the highest plane of consciousness on the strength of his prayer, he enjoys the sweetest intimacy. He claims his Lord as his eternal Friend, his beginningless and endless Friend. When he reaches God inside the very depths of his heart, he enjoys boundless ecstasy and delight in his Beloved Supreme.

Spirituality is the simplification of life. Spirituality is the glorification of life. When we are in the ordinary human life, there are countless problems. Every day we encounter these countless problems, and we find that there is no way to solve these problems or to simplify our complicated human life. But spirituality is our savior. It comes to solve our problems, to simplify our complicated life and to glorify the divine in us. The divine in us is that very thing that wants to expand, illumine and fulfill the Immortal in us.

How do we simplify our life? Is there any specific way to simplify our complicated life? Yes, we can simplify our most complicated life through our power of concentration. When we concentrate on our problems, we come to discover that our power of concentration has actually come from a Source which is infinitely more powerful than all our problems put together. This Source shows us how to simplify our problems. If we can concentrate on our problems even for five fleeting minutes, I wish to tell you from my own experience that this complicated world of ours will not remain complicated.

Once our life of confusion and complication is over, we expect a life of peace, harmony and satisfaction. Unfortunately, this world of ours has everything except one thing: peace of mind. If we have peace of mind, we do not need anything more from this world, from any individual or even from ourselves. How do we get peace of mind? The answer is through spirituality.

Spirituality has a most powerful hero-soldier. The name of that hero-soldier is meditation. If we know how to sincerely meditate for even five minutes early in the morning before the hustle and bustle of life begins, then we enter into a world of serenity, clarity, purity and peace—a world which is flooded with peace. Each individual seeker has the potentiality, the capacity to meditate soulfully. Some may not be able to meditate immediately. It may take a few weeks or a few months of practice. But no individual will forever remain unknowledgeable in the art of meditation. The art of meditation is something inherent in each individual.

Meditation is the way to acquire peace of mind. Once we have peace of mind, then in our day-to-day multifarious activities we shall enjoy boundless satisfaction. In this satisfaction we shall notice progress—gradual, continuous, illumining and fulfilling progress. To walk consciously along the Road of Eternity, what we need is progress. And inside our progress is God the ever-transcending Reality, which is the birthright of each individual seeker here and everywhere.

Peace Is Our Birthright:
How Can We Have It?

There are two kinds of peace: the outer peace and the inner peace. The outer peace is man's compromise. The inner peace is man's fulfillment. The outer peace is man's satisfaction without being satisfied at all. The inner peace is man's satisfaction in being totally and supremely fulfilled.

How can the outer peace have the same capacity as the inner peace? The outer peace can have the same capacity if and when man's creation and God's creation become inseparably one.

What is man's creation? Right now, man's creation is fear. Man's creation is doubt. Man's creation is confusion. What is God's creation? God's creation is Love. God's creation is Compassion. God's creation is Concern.

Fear is the feeblest ant in man. Doubt is the wildest elephant in man. Confusion is the devouring tiger in man. There is no yawning gulf between man's cherished fear and his forced fear. Doubt God, forgiveness is granted. Doubt yourself, your complete destruction is decreed. Yesterday's confusion was the beginning of your insincerity. Today's confusion is the beginning of your insecurity. Tomorrow's confusion will be the beginning of your futility.

God's Love for man is man's aspiration. God's Compassion for man is man's salvation. God's Concern for man is man's perfection.

Man's fulfilling and fulfilled search for the Real is peace. God the Love is man's eternal Guest in the inmost recesses of his heart. God the Peace is man's eternal Host in the inmost recesses of His Heart. That is why we can unfalteringly and unmistakably claim that loving and fulfilling peace is our birthright.

How can we have peace—even an iota of peace—in our outer life, amidst the hustle and bustle of life and our multifarious activities? Easy: we have to choose the inner voice. Easy: we have to control our binding thoughts. Easy: we have to purify our impure emotions.

The inner voice is our guide. Binding thoughts are the dark and unpredictable weather. Impure emotion is the inner storm. We have to listen to the inner voice always. It is our sure protection. We have to be cautious of our binding thoughts. These thoughts have tremendous vitality. We must never allow them to swell into tornadoes. We have to face them and then dominate them. These thoughts are absolutely non-essential, and we have no time to fret over non-essentials. If we want to have inner and outer peace, we have to refrain from the luxury of the emotional storm. Impure emotion is immediate frustration, and frustration is the harbinger of total destruction within and without.

To choose the inner voice, we have to meditate early in the morning. To control and dominate our undivine thoughts, we have to meditate at noon. To purify our unlit, impure emotions, we have to meditate in the evening.

What is meditation? Meditation is man's constant awareness and conscious acceptance of God. Meditation is God's unconditional offering to man.

> Peace is the beginning of love.
> Peace is the completion of truth.
> Peace is the return to the Source.

The Answer to World-Despair

Before we look for the answer to world-despair, let us first try to know why there is world-despair. Only if we do so shall we be able to offer an answer to world-despair. World-despair exists because the world desperately needs life-illumining light. Why is there world-despair? World-despair exists because the world constantly needs life-energizing love. Why is there world-despair? World-despair exists because the world immediately needs life-immortalizing delight.

The answer to world-despair is light. The answer to world-despair is love. The answer to world-despair is delight. We need light to see the Creator within and the creation without. We need love to feel the Beloved within and the Lover without. We need delight to sail God's Boat within and to reach God's Shore without.

World-despair is at once bad and good, undivine and divine. It is bad because it lives in the darkness-ignorance-kingdom. It is good and divine because it cries for light, more light, abundant light and infinite light; love, more love, abundant love and infinite love; delight, more delight, abundant delight and infinite delight.

World-despair exists because there is a yawning gulf between our self-giving and the world's receptivity, between the world's self-giving and our receptivity. World-despair exists because there is a yawning gulf between our life-perfection and God's manifestation, between God's Life-Perfection and our manifestation.

Grace from Above is the only link between our self-giving and the world's receptivity, and between the world's self-giving and our receptivity. Aspiration from below is the only link between our life-perfection and God's manifestation, and between God's Life-Perfection and our manifestation.

The absolute Grace of the Supreme has given birth to the transcendental Reality and the universal Reality. Man's constant inner cry reaches the transcendental Reality, which is the acme of perfection, in the Beyond, and at the same time manifests the universal Reality in the core of each aspiring individual on earth.

In the world of yesterday, ignorance guided and molded us. In the world of today, despair lords it over us. In the world of tomorrow, glowing hope will guide and lead us. In the world of the day after tomorrow, we shall grow into God's Promise, the promise of achievement immortal and infinite.

Talking, lecturing and advising the world can never be an adequate answer to world-despair. The most effective answer to world-despair lies in self-giving. We learn the art of self-giving only after we have learned the art of self-finding. And we learn the art of self-finding only after we have learned the art of meditating on the Inner Pilot, the Supreme. What we call meditation is nothing other than God-discovery, and God-discovery is always a perfect stranger to human despair.

This short talk of mine can give us only 1 percent of the capacity to offer the answer to world-despair. But our sincere, deep and soulful meditation is bound to give us 99 percent capacity to offer the answer to world-despair. Let us all meditate only for light, love and delight. Light will open up our eye that sees. Love will open up our heart that feels. Delight will carry us to our Source, the Supreme.

The Way Ahead

*"The way ahead may be difficult, but the
future of mankind is bright."*

Excerpt from a statement by Joao Teixeira da Motta,
Permanent Mission of Portugal to the United Nations.
From a statement before the Second Committee
of the 31st U.N. General Assembly.

From the spiritual point of view, the way signifies aspiration. Aspiration is the inner flame which ever ascends and transcends, and while ascending and transcending, it illumines our earthly life. The aspiration-flame shows us how to see the Truth, how to feel the Truth and how to grow into the Truth. It helps us see, feel and grow into God's transcendental Vision and God's universal Reality.

There are two ways: the human way and the divine way. The human approach is the approach of separativity; the divine approach is the approach of unity in multiplicity and multiplicity in unity. There the Eternal can grow in the fleeting reality and the Infinite can grow in the finite.

The human way leads us to our destination. In this case the way and the destination are two separate realities. When we speak about *the way ahead*, we feel that the starting point and the journey's goal, or the journey's close, are two different places. When we say that something is ahead, it means that the starting point is here and the reality that we are seeking, the culmination, is elsewhere. This is what our human mind teaches us.

But there is another teacher that we can claim as our own, our very own, and that is our inner eye, the third eye, the eye of God-Light. This eye, which is between our eyebrows and a little above, has a different story to tell us. It tells us that God the cosmic Vision and God the cosmic Reality are one and the same, one and inseparable. When we think of God the Vision, we must realize that we are talking about the cosmic Vision, which embodies Reality itself. And when we think of God the cosmic Reality, we must feel that inside the cosmic Reality is nothing but God, the cosmic Vision. The cosmic Vision is the Reality within us in seed form. And the cosmic Reality is the Vision in its manifested form. In the divine way, the destination and the way are the same. Here there is no sense of separativity. Two thousand years ago the Savior, Christ, taught us, "I am the Way, I am the Goal." He also declared, "I and my father are one." In these two most significant utterances, we can see and feel that the way and the destination are inseparably one.

The way ahead may be difficult. Anything that is as yet unachieved may appear difficult. Difficulty is an experience which we go through before the realization-sun dawns on our devoted and illumined heads, and our aspiring and surrendering hearts.

The future of mankind. Who is man? Man is God yet unrealized. Who is God? God is man yet unmanifested. When it is a matter of realization, man has not yet realized who he eternally is. When it is a matter of manifestation, unfortunately, God remains unmanifested. Therefore, man and God are both incomplete. Man manifests God through his self-giving, and God helps man realize who he eternally is through His self-giving.

But the future of mankind is bright. The future is something that grows in the immediacy of today. The past has given us the capacity to become great. The present is giving us the capacity to become good. The future will give us the capacity to become perfect. When we are great, consciously or unconsciously we want to rule the world and lord it over the world. When we are good, consciously or unconsciously we love the world according to the power of our willingness and our receptivity. When we are perfect, we try to love and serve God the Creator in His entire creation, in His own Way.

The future of mankind is bright. What is bright in our outer life? Inspiration is the only thing that has the light; therefore, inspiration is the only thing that is bright in our outer life. Nothing else in our outer life can claim to be bright. What is bright in our inner life? Aspiration is the only thing that is bright in our inner life. As inspiration is bright in our outer life, so aspiration is bright in our inner life. Without inspiration, the outer life is worse than meaningless; without aspiration, the inner life is worse than useless.

When we have inspiration, we feel that there shall come a day when our inspiration will show us God's Face. When we have aspiration, we discover that a day shall dawn, at God's choice Hour, when our aspiration will show us God's Heart. God's Face is Infinity's Beauty and God's Heart is Eternity's Duty.

Do We Have the Capacity
to Help Others?

Do we have the capacity to help others? Yes, we do. Do we have the capacity to help others in words? Yes, we do. Do we have the capacity to help others in deeds? Yes, we do. Then how is it that we do not help others? We do not help others for various reasons. I wish to cite a few deplorable and painful reasons.

The most deplorable reason is a very simple one. We do not want to see happiness in others; we want only our own happiness. By nature, we human beings are often cruel to one another. By nature, we do not want to see others happy. When we see that others are happy, we feel that our own little world is diminished. The animal in us gets satisfaction from destruction. The human in us gets satisfaction from division and a sense of superiority. But the divine in us gets satisfaction only from oneness. The divine in us knows nothing else save and except oneness.

The main reason that we do not help others is because we do not want to see others happy. This root cause branches into several subsidiary causes. One of the subsidiary causes is that we want the rest of the world to see how important we are. When others come to us for help, we feel that we are superior; we want to feel that we are indispensable. When we come to learn that those same persons have gone to others for help, we feel that we were right in not helping them. We feel that since the other parties did not feel that we were indispensable, since they also went to others, we did the right thing in not helping. In this way we justify our unwillingness to help.

There is human friendship and there is divine friendship. Human friendship says, "Give me; I need." Divine friendship says, "Take me, for I am all yours." The human in us has not only failed us time and again, but it will always fail the ultimate test. The divine in us has always succeeded and will always succeed when it is allowed to come forward and act in and through us. This divine success is nothing short of world-harmony and universal harmony, world-peace and universal peace, world-satisfaction and universal satisfaction.

Divine friendship is founded upon oneness. The source of divine friendship, divine love and divine concern is oneness. For this reason, divine friendship is lasting. On the other hand, human friendship is nothing but a rope of sand. We shall not be far from the truth if we say that most human beings are fair-weather friends. When we are desperate and facing inclement weather, our so-called friends desert us in a twinkling. When we ask someone we feel close to, "Are you my friend?" he says, "Of course I am your friend, but on one condition: that you never ask me for a favor." Then we see another friend and ask him, "Are you my friend?" He says, "Of course I am, but on one condition: that I shall always be superior to you. If you are ready to be my servant at every moment, if you are ready to be at my beck and call, if you are ready to sit at my feet with tremendous admiration, then I will accept you as my friend." When we ask a third so-called friend, "Are you my friend?" he answers, "Of course I am, but on one condition: whenever I am in need, you will immediately come to my rescue. But if ever you are in need, you must not count on me, for I have many, many things to do on earth other than help you. If you want me to be your friend, then your acceptance of me has to be unconditional."

When we look for a friend, we are like a helpless beggar. At that time, God our supreme Source is playing the role of the eternal beggar in and through us. Then God goes to some other individuals and asks them to assist others. He wants to play a different role in and through them: the role of the eternal Giver, the divine Friend. To His wide surprise, He gets no response. But since God is compassionate to the needy, He continues trying to find some individuals who will allow Him to play this role in and through them, some individuals in and through whom He can fulfill the aspiration-life and the desire-life of those in whom He is playing the role of a beggar. Finally, He finds some souls that are receptive. They are more than willing to abide by God's express request and come to the rescue of those who are desperately in need of help.

When a seeker needs help, he can do only one thing: dive deep within and bring to the fore his adamantine will. This adamantine will he shall place at the Feet of the Absolute Supreme. Then the Absolute Supreme grants His all-fulfilling Grace to the adamantine will of the seeker. When the seeker's will and the Supreme's Grace become one and are ready to work together, man's aspiration-world and God's Satisfaction-World make God the Beggar and God the Giver totally fulfilled in both the aspiration-world of earth and the satisfaction-world of Heaven.

Is the Spiritual Life
an Escape from Reality?

An unaspiring man thinks that undying pleasure is the only reality. An aspiring man feels that a divine experience is the only reality. A God-realized man knows that God the Supreme Lover alone has the Reality, and that God the Supreme Beloved alone is the Reality. Reality is also God the fulfilling Light and man the fulfilled life.

The abode of transcendental Fulfillment has three doors: love, freedom and delight. The love-door is open only to he who serves crying humanity. The freedom-door is open only to he who serves struggling humanity. The delight-door is open only to he who serves awakening humanity.

The spiritual life is never an escape from reality. On the contrary, the spiritual life is the conscious and spontaneous acceptance of reality in its totality. For a spiritual seeker, the idea of an escape from reality is absurdity plus impossibility, for spirituality and reality need each other to be supremely fulfilled. Without reality's soul, spirituality is worse than useless. Without spirituality's breath, reality is more than meaningless. Spirituality with reality means man's inner cry for perfect Perfection. Reality with spirituality means God's omnipotent Will for total and absolute manifestation.

Escape is a base thought. Like the worst possible thief, into the heart of tenebrous gloom, escape gains easy and free access. He who indulges in the idea of immediate escape unmistakably commits lingering suicide.

Acceptance, the acceptance of life with a divine attitude, is not only a lofty idea, but the very ideal of life. This ideal of life is realized, revealed and manifested through God's soul-elevating inspiration and man's life-building aspiration.

Acceptance of life is the divine pride of true spirituality. To live a spiritual life is our only responsibility.

Acceptance of life in a divine way is the transcendence of human ego. The transcendence of ego is man's real dignity and true worth. Momentous are the words of former Secretary-General U Thant: "The dignity and worth of the human person is not merely a philosophical concept. It is, and should be, a working principle of human existence guiding our daily lives."

Acceptance of life is the assurance of faith. Faith walks along the road of fulfilling and fulfilled Immortality. Escape from reality will, in the twinkling of an eye, weaken our resolve, loosen our armor of protection and finally throw us into the very depths of the annihilation-sea.

No, those who have chosen spirituality will never make a cowardly escape. We must always be brave. Divine courage is our birthright. We are the hero-warriors of supreme Reality, chosen to fight against the teeming, brooding and threatening ignorance-night.

Western Dynamism
and Eastern Spirituality

Western dynamism lives in its searching mind and manifesting vital. Eastern spirituality lives in its crying heart and illumining soul.

Spirituality is the inner urge of an Eastern seeker to see God face to face and realize God in His totality. Dynamism is the vital urge of a Western seeker to reveal God and manifest God here on earth. Dynamism serves God. Spirituality loves God.

The body's dynamism is regularity. The vital's dynamism is punctuality. The mind's dynamism is clarity. The heart's dynamism is purity. The soul's dynamism is certainty.

The body's spirituality is simplicity. The vital's spirituality is sincerity. The mind's spirituality is humility. The heart's spirituality is spontaneity. The soul's spirituality is Reality.

A dynamic man is quick on his feet to reach his destined Goal, the Goal of the Beyond. A spiritual man is quick with his eagerness to please God, the Inner Pilot, in His own Way.

Dynamism is life's capacity. Spirituality is the soul's necessity. The aura of outer success surrounds a dynamic man. The aura of inner progress surrounds a spiritual man.

A dynamic man is a karma yogi. He devotes himself to the path of action, disinterested action, with implicit devotion and surrendered service to God. A spiritual man is a jnana yogi. He tries to live in the knowledge of God with his awakened and illumined mind and heart. Dynamism invites God. Spirituality receives God. Yoga achieves God.

Western dynamism wants to shoulder the responsibility of saving the entire world. Eastern spirituality tries and cries to know what God's Will is and what God wants.

Western dynamism needs the aspiration of Eastern

spirituality in order to please God in the inner world. Eastern spirituality needs the inspiration of Western dynamism in order to please God in the outer world.

Western dynamism has to learn the secret of Eastern spirituality: God is Love, God is Peace. Eastern spirituality has to learn the secret of Western dynamism: God is the Supreme Warrior, the Supreme Victor over teeming ignorance and darkening death. God needs Western dynamism to offer His Omnipotence-Light to the world at large. God needs Eastern spirituality to offer His Ocean of Love and Peace to the world at large.

Western dynamism and Eastern spirituality are the two wings of God the Eternal Bird, who will carry the message of earth's aspiration to the highest Abode of the Supreme, and who will bring down the message of infinite Compassion from the highest Abode of the Supreme to the aching, crying consciousness of Mother-Earth.

When Western dynamism and Eastern spirituality become inseparably one, God will be known as a fulfilled man, and man will be known as a perfect God.

Why Do I Have to Become Spiritual?

Why do I have to become spiritual? I have to become spiritual precisely because I wish to see something, do something and become something. There are many people on earth who do not feel the necessity of this, and I do not find fault with them. But my inner being tells me that I have to see something, do something and become something.

What I wish to see is perfection in my life and in the life of each and every individual. What I wish to do is to love mankind unreservedly and divinely. What I wish to become is a conscious and chosen instrument of God.

Two lives: a life of aspiration and a life of desire. I have been in the life of desire. In that life I did not have even an iota of peace and bliss. Therefore, I have entered consciously and soulfully into a new life, the life of aspiration. In my desire-life, my existence was tossing on a shoreless sea, and it found its reality on a goal-less shore. In order to swim in the sea of Reality, in order to reach the Golden Shore of the Beyond, I entered into the life of aspiration.

It is a mistake to think that a spiritual person is impractical. On the contrary, a spiritual person is really practical. An ordinary, unaspiring person thinks of God as being in Heaven, millions and billions and trillions of miles higher than his own existence. His God is not near him, not in front of him, but in an unknown or unknowable Heaven.

A spiritual person has a different idea of God. He says, "If God exists, then He has to be inside my heart, all around me, right in front of me." A seeker is practical. He does not accept the theory that God is in a distant and unattainable Heaven, that God is aloof and uninterested in his life. He says, "Only if my God is right here on earth will He be able to fulfill my aspiration and my need."

Once he realizes that God is right in front of him, he immediately feels that God is everywhere, both in Heaven and on earth. When he thinks of God in Heaven, he immediately feels that God is the Dream-fulfilling Reality. And when he thinks of God on earth, he feels that God is the Reality-illumining Dream—Divinity's conscious and ever-transcending Dream, which illumines Reality.

In the ordinary life there are many needs. But in the spiritual life, gradually we come to realize that there is only one need, and that need is to love God. There is also something that is not needed, and that is self-proclamation. When I love God, I feel that I am touching the very root of the God-Tree. And if I touch the root, then the dynamic flowing energy in the root will take me to all the branches, leaves and flowers. But when I proclaim myself, I just limit and bind myself; I am not able to taste, to enjoy myself as a universal Reality. My self-proclamation immediately separates me from the whole, which I once upon a time was, which I want to become and which I eventually will be.

A spiritual person is not only practical, but also normal and natural. Everything in his life is orderly. He goes from one to two to three, and not the other way around. For a normal person, first things come first. What is the first thing? It is God, because God is the Creator, God is the Source. Every day dawns with a new life, a new hope, a new sense of Immortality. When the morning dawns, a seeker does first things first. First he prays to God, then he thinks of mankind and finally he thinks of himself.

When he prays to or meditates on God, the seeker uses the instrument called divine surrender. "Let Thy Will be done," he says. When he thinks of mankind, he uses the instrument called divine love. He uses his divine love-power to become inseparably one with humanity. Finally, when he thinks of himself, he uses his divine discipline-power, his self-control. If he uses his power of self-control, then at every moment a new dream can be dreamt by the divine within him. A higher call from within takes him to his divine reality, which is ever-transcending.

As an individual, I have to know that my physical body is not my only reality. I also have a soul, a heart, a mind and a vital. I have to care for my soul first, because this is the very best part of me. The soul is constantly dreaming in and through me, and the dream of the soul is the harbinger of my conscious self-perfection. So I have to think of the soul or meditate on the soul first.

Next I think of my heart. My heart needs to offer love and it needs to receive love. First it gives love, then it receives love and finally it becomes divine love itself. After giving and receiving love, my heart will feel its inseparable oneness with everything and everyone.

Then I have to be concerned with my mind. I have to meditate on the mind, with the idea of expanding and illumining it. I do not need the mind that binds me, limits me or separates me; I need a mind that will gladly listen to my heart and my soul, a mind that can feel the universal oneness.

After that I have to pay attention to my vital. When I focus on my vital, I have to think of dynamic energy. If there is no dynamic energy, I cannot produce or achieve anything. Life is a river that flows constantly and continuously. Vital energy is the current that carries us to the sea, the sea of illumination and perfection.

Finally, I have to think of the physical. It is the physical that has to serve the dynamic vital, the searching mind and the self-giving heart. It is the physical foundation upon which the manifestation of the all-illumining divine light must take place.

When we become truly spiritual, we can boldly say that what we really need are the heart and soul to guide us through life. Granted, if we want a diamond, we may be able to find a diamond in the mind-room, and we can find the same kind of diamond in the heart-room. But the moment we enter into the mind-room, we see that that room is full of rubbish and undivine things. The diamond is covered, and it will take us days, months and years to uncover it. When we enter into the heart-room, we see that there is nothing else but the diamond. The moment we open the door, the diamond is right there before us.

A spiritual person has wisdom. Just by seeing the diamond, he will not be fully satisfied; he will want to grow into the consciousness of the diamond. This spiritual diamond is perfect Perfection. The spiritual person enters into the heart-room, sees the diamond, touches the diamond, meditates on the diamond and becomes one with the diamond. When he becomes one with the diamond, that means he has become a perfect instrument of God. A seeker's true satisfaction dawns only when he becomes a perfect instrument of the Supreme. At that time, he becomes one with both the earth-consciousness and Heaven-consciousness.

A spiritual person wants to realize unity in diversity, harmony in diversity. In the ordinary life, two human beings constantly contradict each other. When we are beginners in the spiritual life, even our divine qualities may not satisfy us. Let us say one seeker has sincerity and another seeker has humility. Both these qualities are of paramount importance. But the person who has sincerity feels he is not being admired the way his friend is being admired. He feels that the person who has humility is getting more appreciation from others, so the person with sincerity is not happy. The person who has humility feels that the person who is sincere is getting more appreciation and admiration, so his own humility does not give him real satisfaction, either.

But when we go deep within, our divine qualities will not compete with one another. On the contrary, each divine quality will appreciate and enhance every other divine quality. When sincerity enters into humility and offers its inner wealth, immediately humility sees that all the divine qualities are equally valuable in the Eyes of God.

After I become spiritual, what is expected of me? I have to offer myself before God and I have to offer myself before mankind. When I offer myself before God, I shall offer my teeming ignorance, the ignorance of millennia. When I offer myself before mankind, I shall offer my divine love. Love I have to offer before humanity; ignorance I have to offer before God.

The life of a spiritual seeker is not the life of a stagnant pool. It is the life of a fresh spring, a spring of ever-flowing consciousness-light. When the seeker feels that his life is ever-flowing consciousness-light, he feels that Heaven—which is God's Dream—is being manifested on earth, and that earth—which is man's cry—is being transformed into the ceaseless Smile of the Supreme.

Spirituality: Is It Only for
the Chosen Few?

Spirituality: is it only for the chosen few? The answer is at once both affirmative and negative. The blessed aspirants who cry for the transcendental truth, peace and bliss are undoubtedly the chosen few. Nevertheless, all human beings, with no exception, can easily swim in the infinite sea of spirituality. But those who have lesser goals, those who want to be satisfied with an iota of peace, bliss and truth, unfortunately cannot dine with the chosen few in the inner world.

I am afraid the beginners and the budding seekers may, at this point, feel discouraged. Truth to tell, in no way do I intend to throw cold water on their aspiration. On the contrary, I want them to understand that the highest Goal will never be denied them. But it is they who have to cultivate the strongest necessity in the world of their own aspiration, in order to reach the ultimate Beyond.

What prevents them from reaching the Beyond? Their fear. What else? Their doubt. But they must know that fear is the owner only of those who do not believe in God. Since they *do* believe in God, and they *do* have faith in God, they need not and must not be afraid of God's transcendental Height. When they doubt themselves, they underestimate their own divinity, overestimate their ignorance-reality, belittle their inner potentiality and aggrandize their temporary and fleeting insecurity. But when they doubt God, it is as if they are playing with a balloon. Their doubt-balloon is bound to burst before long.

I am sure that the budding seekers have sincere love for God, and I am sure that they have real love for themselves. Their love for God will eventually transform them into perfect beauty supreme. Their divine and fulfilling love for themselves as fully awakened and useful members of the human family will be manifested on earth by God Himself. Their love is their inseparable oneness with God's Light and with their own inner Reality.

Now I must also say a few words about the chosen few. Theirs is the task sublime to realize God's universal and transcendental Consciousness. Theirs is the bounden duty to reveal and fulfill God on earth. Among the chosen few, he is by far the best who unconditionally realizes God, reveals God and manifests God at God's choice Hour, in God's own Way.

The chosen few, when they look forward, find themselves already seated in the Dream-Boat of the Supreme. When they look upward, they find themselves already seated in the Life-Boat of the Supreme. When they look inward, they find themselves already seated in the Soul-Boat of the Supreme.

The Supreme blesses a budding seeker. The Supreme caresses a climbing seeker. The Supreme utilizes a flowering seeker. The Supreme extols a realized seeker to the skies. The Supreme unreservedly offers Himself to the supremely realized seeker who unconditionally serves Him in the heart of humanity.

Spirituality: The Union of Heaven-Vision and Earth-Aspiration

In this world, when someone does not see eye-to-eye with us, we may be tempted to say that he is abnormal and unnatural. We may even go to the length of saying that he is undivine or hostile. This is the division-experience that we unfortunately treasure. But if we pray and meditate soulfully each day, then we come to realize that the most important thing in each person's life is the freedom of his inner life, the freedom to follow his own Inner Pilot. Everyone is being motivated and guided by his Inner Pilot. Just because you do not have the same realization that I have, we cannot call each other abnormal.

Here in God's creation, countless beings are consciously or unconsciously fulfilling God in their own way. But a seeker tries to consciously please and fulfill God in God's own Way. This is the difference between those who aspire and those who do not aspire. Non-seekers try to possess God and utilize God in their own way, whereas seekers try to achieve God's Light to please Him, fulfill Him and manifest Him here on earth in His own Way.

Those who are not crying for God, for Truth or for Light, according to strict inner philosophy, are like dead soldiers in God's army. One need not be dead on the physical plane, but one is inwardly dead if he does not aspire. If his life on earth is spent only in wallowing in the pleasures of ignorance, he is already dead. When there is no aspiration for Light, when there is no interest in progress, then there is no divine satisfaction. That kind of life is nothing short of death.

Earth's understanding of Light is very limited. When we try to judge others or examine others, we immediately lose our sense of identification. But if we focus our attention on all things with the same amount of sympathy, love and concern, we feel inside all things their basic oneness. When I look at my hand, my thumb is considerably different from my little finger. But there is a feeling of oneness between my little finger and my thumb; so when I concentrate on these two parts of my body, I do not consider one abnormal just because one is larger or smaller or differently shaped than the other.

Anything that is contrary to our own experience may seem abnormal to us. But we have to know that the world is singing the song of oneness. God's Unity and God's Multiplicity we have to see as one. God the Creator, God the Preserver and God the Transformer are all one. In each seeker, God is playing the distinctive roles of Creator, Preserver and Transformer. When we see them separately, with our limited consciousness, we become victims of our own limited understanding. If we try to identify only with God the Creator, then without the least hesitation we shall say that God the Transformer is abnormal.

God started His creation with His Silence-Light. From His Silence-Light, His Sound-Might came into existence. The One wanted to become many. He wanted to experience Himself in countless forms, like the seed that eventually grows into a banyan tree. When the seed grows into a huge tree, we see millions of leaves and thousands of fruits and flowers. But it started its journey as one single seed.

The first thing we have to do in our life is pray and meditate. Early in the morning, if we pray to God, we enter into the world of the Source. Then we try to offer the light that we have received from our prayer and meditation to the world around us. First we achieve and then we give. If I do not have any light, then what am I going to give? We have to go from one to two to three. First we have to go to the Root, the Source, the Unity. But the Source needs manifestation; otherwise, it will remain unfulfilled. Next we have to enter into the world of multiplicity. Finally we have to transform the world and bring Heaven's Perfection into the world. Only in this way can we have true satisfaction.

In unity there must be the song of multiplicity. When we enter into the spiritual life, if we ignore the world around us, if we feel the world around us is dirty and undivine and can never be transformed, then we are mistaken. This attitude is unhealthy, abnormal. We have to accept the world around us as our very own, and inside the world we have to see and feel the living Breath and living Presence of God. Then our realization will tell us that the world is absolutely normal, that God is evolving in His own Way in and through the world. You may be flying to your destination in a jet plane and somebody else may be traveling at the speed of an Indian bullock cart. But who is the driver of the bullock cart and who is the pilot of the plane? In both cases it is God. According to His own Will and according to the seeker's evolution, God is using the bullock cart or the jet plane or something in between. And it is also He who is the passenger proceeding towards the destined Goal, His own ever-transcending Height.

Some seekers who are weak feel that if they remain in the world, they will be devoured by earth-ignorance. This kind of seeker feels that the best thing for him to do is to enter into the Himalayan caves, where he will be safe. But this is not the answer to the problem of human weakness. Human beings who have undivine, ferocious qualities may not follow him to the Himalayan caves; but whatever is inside him will follow him, including his unillumined mind, his earth-bound desires and his own animal qualities. These things will play the role of the undivine human beings he has left behind. They will torture him. His body will be in the Himalayan caves all alone, but his mind and his vital will be roaming everywhere. He will meditate for five minutes or half an hour, and then if he does not see an iota of light, or if he does not feel any certainty in his inner life, he will begin to think, "I have come here to the Himalayan caves, but perhaps I am only fooling myself. Perhaps there is no truth, no reality here. Perhaps this is all self-deception."

If we are real seekers of truth, like divine warriors we will face the world and brave the world here and now. Who tries to escape? He who has done something wrong, he who is a culprit. But we have not done anything wrong, so we need not and must not try to escape. We have to feel that the members of society are like the limbs of our body. If even one part of our being is not transformed, then we are not perfect. We have to strike a balance. Spirit will give us realization, but matter offers us the opportunity for manifestation. We have to try to combine the messages of spirit and matter. Only then will we be able to establish the Kingdom of Heaven here on earth.

How can we combine these two? By uniting Heaven-vision with earth-aspiration. When earth-aspiration climbs up high, higher, highest and Heaven-vision descends, there is a place where the two meet. That meeting place is inside our heart of acceptance, our conscious acceptance of both the vision of Heaven and the aspiration of earth.

When we separate earth-consciousness, which is manifestation, from Heaven-consciousness, which is realization, we are totally lost. But when the aspiration of earth and the vision of Heaven are amalgamated, we become chosen instruments of the Absolute Supreme. At that time, our Heaven-free consciousness and earth's aspiring consciousness make us complete, whole and perfect. The idea of abnormality is absurd then. We are normal, natural, spiritual, divine and perfect, for we consciously, devotedly, soulfully and unconditionally unite the vision of our divinity with the aspiration of our humanity.

Salvation, Liberation And Realization

Salvation is God-discovery.
Liberation is God-achievement.
Realization is God-fulfillment.

A man with salvation, a man with liberation, a man with realization: what are they and what are they not? What they are is Reality's smile. What they are not is unreality's cry.

God's pure Compassion
Gives the seeker salvation.
God's sweet Love
Grants the seeker liberation.
God's proud, divine Oneness
Gives the seeker realization.

In the Western world, salvation is everything. In the Eastern world, especially in India, liberation is really something, but realization is everything. Before he achieves salvation, a seeker only hopes and dreams that his Father in Heaven is for him. After he has achieved salvation, he knows this as a reality. Before he achieves liberation, a seeker feels that the Truth abides somewhere, but it is an unknowable place. After he has achieved liberation, he feels that God the Light was unknown and only now has become fully known. Before he attains realization, a seeker feels God's Presence everywhere, in everything, but he does not see God face to face. After he has realized God, his feeling is transformed into seeing. He sees God face to face just as he would see any individual he meets.

When a person gains salvation, God tells him to feel at every moment that he is the instrument and God is the Doer.

To a person who has achieved liberation, God says, "My child, you have worked hard, very hard, to free yourself from the meshes of ignorance. Perhaps you are tired. If you want to take rest, you may take rest. If you want to work, so much the better; but if you don't want to work, no harm. I am still very pleased with you."

A person who has achieved God-realization hears something still different from God. God tells him, "Before, I worked alone for you, for the world, for the universe. Now you have the key to My universal Consciousness. Now you can be My assistant. Now you can feel that My Wealth is your wealth and you can distribute My Wealth as your very own. Your work and My Work are the same: the manifestation of Divinity, the manifestation of Immortality on earth. Together we shall work, together we shall liberate the earth-consciousness. Together we shall transform our Vision into Reality."

He who has achieved salvation, in God's Eye is very good. He who has achieved liberation, in God's Eye is very great. He who has achieved realization, in God's Eye is both very good and very great. A man with salvation feels that God is his Father. A man with liberation feels that God is his Friend. A man with realization feels that God is his All.

Philosophy, Religion and Yoga

Philosophy sees the Truth. Religion feels the Truth. Yoga becomes the Truth. God-Perfection is the Truth.

Philosophy is in the searching mind. Religion is in the loving heart. Yoga is in the aspiring entire being.

A real philosophy teacher teaches the outer world. A real religion teacher loves the inner world. A real yoga teacher discovers his inseparable oneness with both the inner world and the outer world.

The inner world achieves. The outer world reveals. The inner world achieves God-Height. The outer world reveals God-Depth. God-Height is soulfully beautiful. God-Depth is beautifully soulful. When a seeker becomes soulfully beautiful, he embodies the cry of continuous self-transcendence. When a seeker becomes beautifully soulful, he reveals constantly the smile of self-transformation and self-perfection.

The human philosophy ignores the animal in us and belittles the human in us. The divine philosophy accepts the challenges of life, braves the buffets of life and finally, offers life a conscious awareness of its purpose.

Human religion is the song of the unfulfilling and unfulfilled many and the marked and isolated many. Divine religion is the dance of the liberating and liberated, the fulfilling and fulfilled One in the aspiring many, and of the many in the immortalizing and immortal One.

The human yoga needs God because God is great, absolutely great and because He is powerful, eternally powerful. The divine yoga needs God because God is good, in the sound-life of the finite and in the silence-life of the Infinite.

Philosophy is man's close association with God. Religion is man's conscious and close union with God. Yoga is man's conscious, close and constant oneness with God.

Philosophy sees the wisdom in truth. Religion realizes the code of life with truth. Yoga becomes the delight for truth.

Philosophy is often the mind-capacity. Religion is often the heart-capacity. Yoga is always the God-capacity.

Philosophy ascends from the searching mind. Religion ascends from the crying heart. Yoga ascends and descends: ascends for the discovery of the silence-world and descends for the mastery of the sound-world.

Philosophy unmistakably tells the world about its stupendous victory. Religion unreservedly tells the world about its momentous mission. Yoga unconditionally tells the world about its auspicious perfection.

Philosophy is brave. It tries to understand the higher world. Religion is wise. It tries to acknowledge the outer world. Yoga is pure. It tries to accept the higher, the outer and the inner worlds.

Philosophy inspires us to become great. Religion inspires us to become good. Yoga inspires us to become perfect.

Philosophy teaches and teaches. Religion preaches and then practices. Yoga practices and practices.

Philosophy gets untold joy in guiding the world. Religion gets boundless joy in conquering the world. Yoga gets spontaneous joy in serving the world.

The philosophy of the United Nations is to sincerely please all the countries. The religion of the United Nations is to generously help all the countries that are abiding by the principles of truth. The Yoga of the United Nations is to sleeplessly turn the entire world into a peaceful and soulful oneness-home.

The Seeker's Mind

O mind, what are you doing to me? You are destroying all my divine possibilities. You are delaying indefinitely my supreme inevitabilities.

O mind, what are you doing to me? I thought that you would teach my vital and my body—the younger members of our family—how to enjoy the strength of vastness. Alas, instead of doing that, you are teaching them how to enjoy the weakness of meanness.

O mind, what are you doing to yourself? I thought that you were wise enough to see and feel the happiness that my heart enjoys by becoming inseparably one with the soul and its unfathomable ecstasy. Alas, instead of doing that, you are enjoying base jealousy towards the heart.

O mind, what have I done to you? My human life is for happiness. The moment you think of me, all my happiness disappears. The moment I think of you, I suffer the same fate.

O mind, why, why on earth do you have to be so cruel to me? You torture me ruthlessly! I forgive you unreservedly, but alas, I am unable to forget you, your jealousy, your meanness, your destructiveness. Deathless have become my excruciating pangs.

O mind, cruelty incarnate, you have bound me taut to your pitch-dark, tenebrous and tiny world. As if that is not enough, you are strangling me there. Death is undoubtedly preferable to the untold torture that you continuously inflict upon me. Truth to tell, you have been punishing me since you have known me with your doubt-dart and suspicion-gun. In you, meanness has reached its zenith. In you, jealousy plays with the darkest night. In you, insecurity fails to see the face of purity's beauty.

O mind, you are nothing but your own unparalleled stu-pidity. Even when God Himself with His infinite Compassion-Light enters into your sordid existence for its radical transfor-mation and perfect perfection, you suspect God openly, strongly and unreservedly. Your fertile and futile imagination instigates you to think that God has an ulterior motive. Not only do you know what a suspicion-snake is, but you are nothing but that and that alone.

Helpless, God enters into His own birthless and deathless Reality—transcendental Height and universal Delight—to hear one solitary message: "Endless patience, endless patience."

God the Compassion is not enough to transform you. God the Patience is needed, too.

O mind, some retribution you richly deserve. I give you my word of honor, with God the Pilot Supreme as the witness, that I shall ultimately compel you to become eternally one with my heart, which enjoys inseparable oneness-delight with Infinity's Light, Eternity's Peace and Immortality's Love.

The Inner Call

Sometimes the inner call is a tempting one. Sometimes the inner call is an illumining one. For those who are not sincere, the inner call is temptation. But for those who are sincere, the inner call is always illumination. On the basis of the inner call, we make a choice.

When we get the inner call, very often we notice a few conflicting forces. These forces are from the desire-life and from the aspiration-life. The forces of the desire-life tell us that we are under obligation to remain with them, since for many, many years they have fed us, nourished us and fulfilled us according to their capacity. But the forces of aspiration tell us that only a new kind of life, a new kind of inner nourishment, can give us happiness and satisfaction. If we accept the call of aspiration, then we begin walking along the path of illumination. If we do not accept the call of aspiration, we may feel that the forces of aspiration are nothing but temptation-forces. We feel that we are being invited by the unknown and that we may be totally swallowed by the unknown.

Based on the inner call, we make a choice. Sometimes we make a choice to become good. Then we have to decide how far we want to go with the call. In order to become good, we have to give up quite a few old things, and we have to accept and adopt quite a few new things. But we have to feel that the things we are giving up are not worth having, since they have not given us fulfillment or satisfaction. At the same time, there are things that are worth keeping from our old way of life. Those things that can be transformed, illumined and perfected, we shall not give up.

The day after tomorrow is the fourth of July, a day which is most significant in the development not only of America, but also of the entire world. Two hundred years ago there was a significant call that came directly from the Absolute Supreme, the call for America's independence. The inner beauty, the inner light and the inner perfection of that call were received by awakened Americans and by the world at large.

Always there is an inner call going out to humanity from the Divine. This call will come to different individuals on different planes of consciousness. When we hear that call, we have to know how far we want to follow it on the physical plane, on the vital plane, on the mental plane, on the psychic plane. Each plane is limitless, so it is we who have to decide how far to go according to our capacity and receptivity. No matter on which plane the inner call comes, once we start our journey, we should not turn back. Some people want only to start their journey, while others want to walk a considerable distance, and still others want to reach the destination. Again, there will be a few who will not be satisfied even when they reach the destination. They want to come back to the starting point again to teach others how to walk forward to reach the goal.

Seekers who follow the inner call ultimately reach God. Some do so on the strength of a mutual agreement with this inner call. They feel that they will give what they can give, and they will receive from God what God can give. Again, there are some seekers who reach God on the strength of their conscious, constant surrender to their inner call. They tell God that they will do everything unconditionally right from the beginning to the end. God is extremely pleased with these seekers, both in Heaven and on earth.

Even those who are very bad students in the aspiration-world are far better than those who are still living only in the desire-world. If we totally give up the world of aspiration and go back to the ordinary world, to the desire-life, then we are going back to the plane where there is no satisfaction. Just because the inner plane is not giving us satisfaction in our own way, we should not go back to the plane where we have seen that there is no satisfaction at all. We have to continue from where we are. Today I may not be getting nectar to drink, but shall I then drink filthy, dirty water? Since my goal is to drink nectar, I shall not go back and be satisfied with dirty water, even if I cannot drink nectar today. No, I will go on trying to get nectar.

When we hear the inner call, no matter where we are, we have to go forward. Even if we feel that we are already standing at the head of the line, we have to go forward. When we go forward because of an inner call, it means a special blessing has descended upon us. If we do not avail ourselves of this opportunity, it may take a number of years, a whole lifetime or quite a few incarnations before we get another call. To receive a call is not like receiving an earthly meal. If we have missed lunch, we know we will get supper after three or four hours. But once we miss an inner call, we may have to wait for centuries before we get the opportunity for that kind of inner nourishment again. An earthly meal satisfies us for two or three hours. But the inner satisfaction that we get from following the inner call will last for centuries. We can live for Eternity on the inner nourishment we get when we listen to the inner call.

When the Buddha received the inner call, you could say that already he had everything. He was a prince; he had a beautiful wife, a child, a kingdom. He had wealth, power, world-enjoyment, everything. The world of desire was all around him. But he gave all this up when the inner call came.

For Sri Aurobindo, the call first came when he was serving as a professor. From that call he entered into the world of politics. Then another call came, and he gave up politics and entered into the world of spirituality.

In Swami Vivekananda's case, in spite of being well-educated according to Western standards, when the inner call came, he offered his life at the feet of someone who did not care for earthly knowledge or education at all, but who could nourish him spiritually. There was considerable conflict in his life, and at times he tried to go back to the ordinary life. But his inner call was so powerful that in spite of this conflict, he continued to move forward in his spiritual life.

Once we listen to the inner call and accept the inner life, we totally change the course of our development. Those who are here are all seekers. True, we have all kinds of weaknesses and defects, but from the strict spiritual point of view, we are not merely human beings. Once we accept the spiritual life, we need never think of ourselves as mere human beings. The moment we heed the inner call, we become aspiring divine beings. Of course, there are grades of divinity. In the world of divinity, somebody can be more divine than somebody else. There will be some who do not yet take God seriously, who do not take Truth seriously, who do not take Light seriously. There will be others who do take God seriously, but their seriousness is not always constant. When we are in the spiritual life, ultimately we have to take our inner commitment seriously and we have to take our dedication to God seriously at every moment.

Each individual has God inside him. When he realizes the Highest, each individual will realize that God's Vision is nothing but Wisdom-Light. God created the world with His inner Vision, and this Vision is all Wisdom. Wisdom is not mere intelligence or cleverness; wisdom is something entirely different. Believe it or not, Wisdom is understanding and compassion. God's Wisdom and God's Compassion are one and the same thing. Because of His Compassion, God is using His Wisdom for us. And because of His Wisdom, God is using His Compassion for us. When we listen to the inner call, we consciously receive God's Compassion and grow into God's Wisdom.

Right now we are all at the United Nations. The United Nations is the offspring of the League of Nations. President Wilson heard an inner call, and because of his inner call he tried and cried, cried and tried to create a union of the world's nations. Now the League of Nations has truly become a world body, which we call the United Nations. The United Nations also has an inner call. That inner call is from the soul of the world, not from the body of individual nations. It does not come from the geography of the world or the history of the world; it comes from the inner reality of the world. The geography of the world will say one thing about the U.N. The history of the world will say another thing about the U.N. But the living inner reality of the world will say something else. The living inner reality says that the role of the U.N. is to serve not individuals as such, not nations as such, but the cry that is inside the world, the cry that is inside each human being on earth.

An inner call comes to awaken us, to illumine us. It makes us feel that just because God the infinite Truth, God the infinite Light is inside us, we can hope and try and cry to become inseparably one with God. We use the term "hope" because we may not immediately have much faith, either in God or in ourselves. When we have sincere faith in ourselves, we come to see the source of that faith. We see that our faith comes from the Supreme, from the highest Absolute. If we know that we have a Source which has boundless peace, light and bliss for us, then we can go forward confidently. But we have faith that we can and shall move forward, precisely because we know that we have a Source that is more than willing to lead us forward to the ever-transcending Vision-World and Reality-World.

It is from the inner call that we make a choice, it is from the inner call that we move forward, and it is from the inner call that we eventually realize the Highest. And after we realize the Highest, we feel that if anything remains unillumined anywhere on earth, then the main purpose of realization, which is satisfaction, we have not achieved. Everything must be illumined and perfected. Only then can we have perfect satisfaction. We go from call to choice, from choice to destination, and from destination to more inner aspiration for the ever-transcending Goal.

Spirituality: The Fount of World-Peace

Spirituality is aspiration. Spirituality is yoga. When we have learned what we can expect from aspiration and what we can expect from yoga, world-peace will no longer remain a far cry. Aspiration is a seeker's conscious longing for a higher reality. Yoga is a seeker's conscious oneness with God.

Aspiration leads us to seek God-consciousness. Yoga offers God-consciousness to us. Aspiration takes us inward to the ultimate Source. Yoga inundates our consciousness with the light, peace, bliss and power of the Beyond.

Why do we aspire? We aspire because we love God and want God to love us. When we aspire, we go far beyond the domain of the physical mind and sit at the Feet of God the Light.

Why do we practice yoga? We practice yoga in order to feel consciously that God is our very own. We practice yoga because we feel that our fulfillment on earth can take place only when we have realized, revealed and manifested God's Divinity and Reality here on earth. When we practice yoga, we dive deep within, and there we see God and talk to Him face to face.

He who has no aspiration can never free himself from stark ignorance. He who does not practice yoga can neither receive nor achieve boundless light.

As human beings we have two major instruments: one is the mind, the other is the heart. Very often the mind that we use is the doubtful mind, and the heart we use is the fearful heart. Unfortunately, the doubtful mind can never aspire, and the fearful heart can never practice yoga.

True aspiration and teeming human limitations never go together. True yoga and the life of unlit pleasure cannot go together. Constant aspiration and all-fulfilling divinity can and must go together. The highest type of yoga, which is conscious surrender to God's Will, always goes together with the Life of God.

Aspiration tells us that we will be able to see the Truth of the Beyond. Yoga goes one step further. Yoga tells us that the Truth of the Beyond is within us. Finally, God comes and tells us, "My child, you are the Truth of the Beyond. You are My Beyond."

Spirituality is the fount of world-peace. Spirituality is the fulfillment of all responsibilities. This is because Divinity is the birthright of spirituality. When an individual touches the foot of a tree, his consciousness enters into the tree—into the branches, the leaves, the fruits and the flowers. In the spiritual sense, God is the tree, while the leaves, flowers and fruits are human beings. When you touch the Feet of God, your very consciousness enters into His universal Consciousness and into the infinite beings of His manifestation.

Each individual has his own way of achieving peace. A child finds peace when he is running around outside. An unillumined adult finds peace when he feels that he can lord it over others. In the evening of his life, an old man thinks that he will find peace if the world recognizes his greatness or offers its gratitude to him. But peace can never dawn on any individual if it is not properly sought. The child cannot achieve true peace by running around in the street. He soon finds frustration in this so-called fulfillment. A day will come when he will pray to God for a calm and quiet life. Then he will begin to discover peace. If an adult wants to have real peace, he has to realize that he cannot get it by possessing the world or governing the world. It is only by offering what he has and what he is to the world, consciously and unreservedly, that he will find peace. The old man who will soon pass behind the curtain of Eternity can have peace only if he does not expect anything from the world. Then his inner consciousness and outer being will be flooded with peace. World-peace will begin when human expectation ends.

World-peace can come into existence when each individual and each nation consciously feel that other human beings and other nations do not depend on them. No nation is indispensable. But if one nation helps another devotedly and unconditionally, then the world will be inundated with fulfilling peace.

Spirituality is the fulfillment of all responsibility. To love the world is our responsibility. To serve the world is our responsibility. Unfortunately, when we think of the world, we do not think of it in a divine or proper way. The world immediately misunderstands us, and we find it impossible to have an inner understanding with the world. It is like a mother and son. In spite of her best intention, the mother finds it difficult to please the son because she thinks of him in her own way and likewise, the son understands the mother in his own way. Because of this lack of communication, the mother and the son get no joy in fulfilling their mutual responsibilities.

We have to love the world; it is our responsibility. But what happens when we attempt to fulfill our responsibility to the world? We try to possess and bind the world, and while we are doing this we see that we have already been bound and possessed by the world. We have a sublime opportunity to fulfill our responsibility to the world, but we badly misuse it.

We want to please the world, but how can we please the world if we are not pleased with our own lives? It is sheer absurdity to try to please others if we are not pleased with our inner and outer existence. God has given us big mouths, and we try to please others with our words. But inside our hearts there is often a barren desert. If we have no inner peace, joy or love, how can we offer these things to the world? How can we offer anything divine if we do not practice what we preach? Spirituality offers us the capacity to practice what we preach. If we do not follow the path of spirituality, we shall only preach. But if we really practice yoga, we shall also live the truths that we speak about.

How can we fulfill all our responsibilities? We have tried in human ways, but we have failed. We think of the world with good will, but the world remains exactly the same as it was yesterday. We love the world, but the world still remains full of cruelty and hatred. We try to please the world, but the world does not want to be pleased. It is as if the world has taken a vow that it will not allow itself to be pleased. Why does all this happen? It is because we have not pleased our Inner Pilot first. If we have no determination to please our Inner Pilot, how can we offer the world peace, joy and love? Unless and until we have pleased the Inner Pilot, the world will always remain a battlefield where the soldiers of fear, doubt, anxiety, worry, imperfection, limitation and bondage will fight; and consciously or unconsciously, we will play with these undivine soldiers.

Deep within us, divinity is crying to come to the fore. The divine soldiers are simplicity, sincerity, purity, humility, surrender to God's Will and feeling of oneness. These soldiers are more than ready and eager to fight with fear, doubt, anxiety and worry. Unfortunately, we do not consciously identify ourselves with the divine soldiers; we consciously or unconsciously identify ourselves with the undivine soldiers, and that is why world-peace is still a far cry. World-peace can be achieved, revealed, offered and manifested on earth when the divine power of love replaces the undivine love of power.

> When the power of love
> Replaces the love of power,
> Man will have a new name: God.

READER/CUSTOMER CARE SURVEY

If you are enjoying this book, please help us serve you better and meet your changing needs by taking a few minutes to complete this survey. Please fold it & drop it in the mail. **As a thank you, we will send you a gift.**

Name: _____

Address: _____

_____

Tel. # _____

Gender: ____ Female ____ Male

Age: ____ 18-25   ____ 46-55
____ 26-35   ____ 56-65
____ 36-45   ____ 65+

Marital Status: ____ Married ____ Single
____ Divorced ____ Partner

Is this book: ____ Purchased for self?
____ Purchased for others?
____ Received as gift?

How did you find out about this book?

____ Catalog
____ Store Display
Newspaper
____ Best Seller List
____ Article/Book Review
____ Advertisement
Magazine
____ Feature Article
____ Book Review
____ Advertisement
____ Word of Mouth
____ T.V./Talk Show (Specify) _____
____ Radio/Talk Show (Specify) _____
____ Professional Referral _____
____ Other (Specify) _____

What subject areas do you enjoy reading most? (Rank in order of enjoyment)

____ Women's Issues   ____ New Age
____ Business Self Help   ____ Aging
____ Relationships   ____ Altern. Healing
____ Inspiration   ____ Parenting
____ Soul/Spirituality   ____ Diet/Nutrition
____ Recovery   ____ Exercise/Health
____ Other (Specify) _____

What do you look for when choosing a personal growth book? (Rank in order of importance)

____ Subject   ____ Author
____ Title   ____ Price
____ Cover Design   ____ In Store Location
____ Other (Specify) _____

When do you buy books? (Rank in order of importance)

____ Xmas   ____ Father's Day
____ Valentines Day   ____ Summer Reading
____ Birthday   ____ Thanksgiving
____ Mother's Day
____ Other (Specify) _____

Where do you buy your books? (Rank in order of frequency of purchases)

____ Bookstore   ____ Book Club
____ Price Club   ____ Mail Order
____ Department Store   ____ T.V. Shopping
____ Supermarket   ____ Airport
____ Health Food Store ____ Drug Store
____ Gift Store   ____ Other (Specify)

Additional comments you would like to make to help us serve you better.

_____

_____

_____

357X/272

Thank You !!

FOLD HERE

3

Secrets
of the
Inner Life

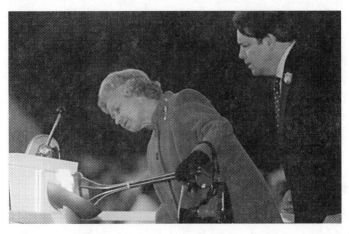

Queen Elizabeth lights a beacon of hope and peace with the Sri Chinmoy Peace Torch on May 8, 1995 to celebrate the 50th anniversary of VE Day in Europe. Peace run participants from each of the four capital cities of the United Kingdom brought the flaming torch to the ceremony in London's Hyde Park before more than 200,000 people.

Her Majesty Queen Elizabeth II
The Queen of the United Kingdom
May 8, 1995

"We are honored to receive you in our country. You have come to us as a true Ambassador of Peace."

His Majesty King Birendra Bir Bikram Shah Dev
The King of Nepal
December 22, 1994

Is the Right to Happiness a Human Right?

Is the right to happiness a human right? First of all, we have to know what happiness is. Happiness is something that feeds our heart, inspires our mind, energizes our vital and illumines our body.

When the heart is happy, it embraces the whole world. When the mind is happy, it accepts the world as its very own. When the vital is happy, it offers its very existence to the world. And when the body is happy, it serves the world the way the world wants to be served.

Our happiness-moon smiles sweetly, charmingly and soulfully when our hope-kite flies in the skies of Divinity's Heights. Our happiness-sun shines brightly when our dream-boat touches the Reality-Shore.

Possession gives birth to human happiness. Renunciation gives birth to divine happiness. Acceptance of God's Will in God's own Way gives birth to supremely divine happiness.

In the domain of teeming fear, happiness bitterly cries. In the sea of brooding doubt, happiness instantly dies. In the domain of lifeless hope, happiness is theoretical and fruitless. In the sea of selfless love, happiness is practical and fruitful.

An aspiring man spreads happiness wherever he goes. An unaspiring man strangles happiness wherever he roams.

The life of happiness is aspiration. The soul of happiness is realization. The goal of happiness is perfection.

Is the right to happiness a human right? Without the least possible hesitation I venture to answer this question in the affirmative. Each man has a soul. Each man has a goal. His soul silently tells him that his perennial Source is all happiness. His goal lovingly tells him that in his constant God-manifestation is his own happiness.

Happiness is *in* God. Happiness is *of* God. Happiness is *for*

119

God. A life of dedication knows that happiness is *in* God. A life of transformation knows that happiness is *of* God. A life of liberation knows that happiness is *for* God.

God's Possession is happiness. Man's achievement is happiness. God's Invention is happiness. Man's discovery is happiness. Man has every right to achieve God's Possession, for that is precisely what God wants man to do. Man has every right to discover God's Invention, for that is precisely what God wants man to grow into. What is God's supreme Possession? Peace. What is God's supreme Invention? Love.

God's supreme Possession is Peace. A peace-loving man is a quarter-God. A peace-achieved man is a half-God. A peace-revealing and peace-spreading man is a full God. A peace-loving man is the serving God. A peace-achieved man is the glowing God. A peace-revealing and peace-spreading man is the fulfilling God in earth-bound time.

God's supreme Invention is Love. He who consciously loves God radiates the highest Divinity. He who soulfully loves God manifests the inmost Divinity. He who unconditionally loves God lives in the ever-radiating, ever-manifesting and ever-transcending Divinity of the Beyond.

A human God-lover achieves God's constant Happiness. A divine God-lover embodies God the Happiness. A human God-lover still has a sense of separativity, so he achieves God's Happiness according to his capacity and according to his receptivity. But a divine God-lover, on the strength of his inseparable and constant oneness with God, embodies God the infinite Happiness.

Why Is It Easier to Disbelieve
than to Believe?

Why is it easier to disbelieve than to believe?

It is easier to disbelieve than to believe because disbelief is an act of descent, whereas belief is an act of ascent. Descending is easier than ascending.

It is easier to disbelieve than to believe because disbelief is an act of breaking, whereas belief is an act of building. Building is more difficult than breaking.

It is easier to disbelieve than to believe because disbelief is an act of our self-centered mind, whereas belief is an act of our self-giving heart.

Disbelief begins its journey in the doubting mind and ends in the destructive vital. Belief begins its journey in the illumining soul and continues to march in the vast kingdom of the aspiring heart.

In disbelief the question arises. In belief the answer dawns.

A man of disbelief, with his eyes firmly closed, tells us what others are, what the world is and what he himself can do for the entire world if he wants to. A man of belief, with his heart's door wide open, tells us what God has done for him, what God is doing for him and what God will do for him.

Disbelief has a perfection of its own. Disbelief finds its perfection in the cyclone of separation. Belief has a perfection of its own. Belief finds its perfection in the music of universal oneness.

Disbelief tells the world, "Be careful, be careful! If not, I shall devour you." Belief tells the world, "Come in, come in, please! I have been eagerly waiting for you."

The human eyes most often believe only themselves; they do not believe others. The human ears most often believe others, even if it is the worst possible gossip. But the divine heart believes in God, in mankind and in its own aspiration.

A man of disbelief hates the world. Why? He feels that the world is never *of* him and can never be *for* him. A man of disbelief always feels that this world does not belong to him and that he can never lord it over the world. This is precisely why a man of disbelief dares to hate the world.

A man of belief loves the world. Why? He believes that this world of ours is verily the aspiring Body of God, the glowing Dream of God and the fulfilling Reality of God.

In the spiritual life, if one cherishes disbelief, one is simply lengthening the distance to the ultimate Goal. But if a seeker has abundant belief in his spiritual life, in his own quest for the ultimate Truth, then undoubtedly he is shortening the distance. Finally, if his inner being is surcharged with boundless faith, then he feels that it is not he who is trying to reach the Goal, but the Goal itself, the Goal of the Beyond, that is running towards him.

There comes a time when a man of disbelief, being totally frustrated, wants to kill the world around him out of exasperation. To his wide surprise, he sees that the wild ignorance of the world has already stabbed him. With his proud knowledge he wants to kill the world; but before he can kill the world, the world, with its wild ignorance, kills him.

A man of belief wants to love the world. To his wide surprise, he sees that his entire existence is in the very heart of the world. The world has already placed a throne in the inmost recesses of its heart for the man of belief to sit upon.

In our spiritual life, disbelief is nothing short of a crime. When we disbelieve, we pour slow poison into our system. It is we who kill our own possibility and potentiality. It is we who wallow consciously and deliberately in the pleasures of ignorance.

Unfortunately, in the lives of some spiritual Masters, disbelief firmly and powerfully knocked at their door before their highest illumination dawned. Finally, by God's Grace, they overcame this disbelief. Again, other spiritual giants were blessed with belief right from the beginning of their spiritual journey.

Why do we disbelieve? We disbelieve because we are afraid of oneness, afraid of the Vast. We feel that when we enter into the Vast, we lose our identity, we lose our individuality, we lose our very existence. But we forget the undeniable Truth that our entrance into the Vastness is nothing short of the enlargement of our divinized consciousness.

For an ordinary person, an unaspiring human being, it is extremely difficult not to disbelieve. A seeker finds it infinitely easier to believe the Truth, the Reality, for his is the life of conscious awareness. An unaspiring person feels that there is something without that is pulling him backwards to bondage, to the unknown. An aspiring seeker knows that there is something within that is pushing him forward to the Light, to the Reality.

When we consciously disbelieve someone, we do not realize the fact that the inner magnet within us pulls the undivine qualities of that person into us. What happens when a person has achieved something, but we do not believe it? The person and his achievement remain the same whether we believe him or not. But the person also has imperfection, limitation and impurity. Our disbelief is a magnet that pulls only the imperfections of the human being in question. But if we offer our belief, then we have within us a magnet that draws the good qualities, the divine qualities, the illumining qualities of the other person.

When we disbelieve God, when we disbelieve the Reality, God remains the same for the Truth-seekers and Truth-lovers. But ignorance gets the opportunity to envelop us, the disbelievers, more powerfully and more completely. When we believe in God, God's Compassion gets the utmost opportunity to work in and through us most powerfully.

The deeper we enter into the spiritual life, the more we become aware of the respective capacities of disbelief and belief. Disbelief is nothing short of destruction, whereas belief is nothing short of a new creation. Each time we believe in something, we see the face of a new creation within and without. And when we go one step ahead, when our inner faith looms large, then we see within ourselves a perfected man and a liberated soul.

Again, when we dive deep within, we see that the time will eventually come for the so-called man of disbelief also to knock at the door of realization. Let him disbelieve to his heart's content; let him run with his disbelief towards his self-chosen destruction. When he is about to reach the door of destruction, God's omnipotent Compassion will send him back to the starting point to begin his march towards the real goal. Even if the man of disbelief is proceeding on the wrong path, let him march! Let him not remain inert. Let the world judge him, let the world offer its comment. A day will dawn when the man of disbelief will come to the right path.

In the spiritual life, in the life of aspiration, in the life of inner awakening, even if one does not have abundant belief or faith in oneself, one need not and must not be doomed to disappointment. Let the disbeliever feel that he is sick, he is weak, he needs treatment, he needs care. Let him see that there are people who are physically strong, vitally strong, mentally strong and psychically strong, and let him mix with these people. If he sincerely wants to see the face of the ultimate Goal, then let him mingle with a man of belief even for a fleeting hour daily. Then he will see the power of belief, the power of inner faith.

We start our life's journey with belief. Then, when the mind starts functioning, disbelief, like a thief, secretly enters into our system. A child always believes his parents. To him, everything that his parents say is true, unquestionably. But when he enters into adolescence, his questioning and doubting mind begins to work. Then he says, "Why? How?" These are the questions that enter into his mind. At that time it is easier for him to believe even the impossible than to believe something that is possible, natural and quite obvious. This is what we observe in our adolescent life.

Opportunity once again knocks at our door during our

youth when we see that the mind has not given us any real satisfaction. When we realize that the mind, with its suspecting and doubting, has not given us even a moment's satisfaction, we want to walk along another road. That is the road of the heart, the aspiring heart, the self-giving heart. While following the path of the heart, we enter into the realm of spirituality. Gradually the lotus within our heart begins to bloom, petal by petal. Each time a petal blooms, we see that our inner divinity is being manifested more and more.

Finally, there comes a time when we see a thousand-petalled lotus fully blossomed within us. At that time we consciously observe our Divine Pilot, our Divine Comrade, our Eternal Friend, the Supreme, right in front of us. He makes us see and feel that, throughout Eternity, we shall be not only *with* Him, but also *for* Him. In our conscious awareness of His Presence, in our conscious feeling of inseparable oneness with Him, we shall establish here on earth, here and nowhere else, the Kingdom of Light, Truth, Peace and Delight.

Does Belief Come Spontaneously or by Effort?

Belief comes spontaneously. Again, belief comes by effort. A sincere seeker, an advanced seeker and a surrendered seeker can and will have spontaneous belief. Belief by effort, personal effort without the divine Grace, without God's unconditional Protection, cannot be as effective as spontaneous belief.

Spontaneous belief is a gift of God for the human in us to see, to feel and to grow into the very image of God. Belief by personal effort is an earthly human discovery, although to some extent it is also necessary.

Believing is seeing. Seeing is believing. When believing is seeing, a seeker becomes a perfect instrument for the Supreme to use in His own Way. When seeing is believing, a seeker makes a solemn promise both to God and to himself that he will realize God and he will fulfill God on earth, but there is no certainty, no guarantee. He may, but he may not. He may not fulfill his divine promise, for at any moment during his long journey he may be assailed by teeming doubts, fears, worries, anxieties and ignorance-night.

Belief by effort is the acceptance, the mere acceptance, of truth and light, and this belief is usually mental and intellectual. But spontaneous belief is conscious and constant oneness with Truth and Light. It is not that belief by personal effort is of no use; this belief has its own value, but it is not as strong and sure as spontaneous belief.

Some people do not have belief; they want to follow the negative path. No matter how far they go, their minds tell them that there is no God. Alas, they will not have even temporary satisfaction on this earth, not to speak of abiding satisfaction. A day will dawn when they will feel that their lack of belief, their denial of God, is not giving them what they want, and then they will be compelled to look for a fulfilling belief.

Not only ordinary human beings, but also many spiritual giants have suffered from doubt and other undivine qualities in their human nature before devotedly and wholeheartedly launching onto the spiritual path. So we must not be doomed to disappointment when we are assailed by doubts in our spiritual life. Belief that comes from within is at the head of the divine spiritual army, and this army destroys our doubts, or rather, let us say it illumines our doubts, perfects our imperfections and transforms our limitation and bondage into divine plenitude.

We have two principal organs: the eye and the ear. Our ordinary human eyes quite often, if not always, believe themselves. Our ears very often believe others. But the divine eye, the third eye, will believe only in the vision of Divinity, and the divine ears will believe only in the truth of Reality. When we listen to the inner command, when we have the capacity to grow into constant obedience to our Inner Pilot, we feel within and without the presence of spontaneous belief. This belief is the reality of our inner obedience. This is divine belief, spontaneous belief. Belief by effort, on the other hand, is a restricted, disciplined human understanding.

Belief is power. A real seeker of the infinite Truth knows this. An insincere and unaspiring seeker is aware of the truth that belief is power, but he cannot go beyond understanding or awareness; whereas a sincere, genuine, devoted and surrendered seeker knows that belief is dynamic power, and he *has* this power as his very own.

A tree bears flowers, and soon afterwards we see fruits. The flower is the harbinger of the fruit. In the spiritual life, belief is the flower. Belief is a divine angel which enters into us as the harbinger of the Lord Supreme.

We can cultivate belief. If we do not have belief, we can develop belief by mixing with sincere spiritual people who care more for God than for pleasure, and with those who care *only* for God in others. When we at last have belief, we can walk with God in His Garden of Light and Delight.

Again, in the spiritual life, spontaneous belief need not and cannot be the last word. There is something infinitely higher and deeper than belief, and that is faith. When we have belief, we can make tremendous progress for a day or for a month or for a year. But then, if we unconsciously or consciously become a victim to undivine forces, our belief loses its strength and we can no longer make fast progress in the spiritual life. The strength of belief, even spontaneous belief, is not enough to take us to the ultimate Goal. Belief is like a child's instrument that we can play for a limited number of hours or years. But when we have faith, we come to realize that we are eternal players and at the same time we are eternal instruments. Later, when we go farther and deeper in our spiritual life, we come to realize that the Player is the Lord Supreme Himself and we are His instruments. He is the eternal Player and we are eternally His chosen instruments.

Spontaneous belief will make us feel what we eternally are: God's chosen children. But if we do not have faith, we will not have the abiding satisfaction of feeling that we are eternally one with Him, that we represent the Absolute Supreme and that our very presence on earth is the manifestation of the Absolute Supreme. It is only when both our outer being and our inner being are surcharged with faith that we can manifest God here on earth.

Faith in ourselves and faith in God must run together. If we say that we have no faith in ourselves but have all faith in God, then we cannot go very far. We have to have faith, constant faith and abundant faith, not only in God, but also in ourselves as God's sons and daughters. When we truly feel that we are God's children, we will find that it is beneath our dignity to make friends with ignorance. Reality, Eternity, Immortality and Infinity will no longer be vague terms; we shall see that they are our birthright. When we have that kind of faith, God will shower His choicest Blessings upon our devoted heads and surrendered hearts.

Again, faith in ourselves must not exceed its own boundary. True, we have to have faith, constant faith, in abundant measure.

But we must also remember the source of our faith. Otherwise, we may think that we are working so hard for our realization of the absolute Truth, for our perfection, all thanks to our own effort. We may feel that 1 percent of the work will be done by the Grace of the Supreme, and 99 percent will be achieved by our personal effort. But when that most auspicious day dawns and we realize the Absolute, we shall see that just the opposite is true: our faith enabled us to contribute 1 percent of personal effort towards our realization, and God supplied the other 99 percent as His divine, unconditional Grace. Then, when we are about to manifest our realization, another truth, a higher and more profound truth, will dawn upon us. At that time we shall realize that the one percent of faith we had, which was absolutely necessary, was also God's Gift to us.

We have to feel that we were chosen from among countless people to run towards the Light. Others are still fast asleep. It was sheer Grace, God's unconditional Grace, that inspired us to come out of ignorance and look towards the Light. Since it was He who inspired us and invited us to join consciously in His cosmic Game, we have to feel that the one percent of faith we had in the beginning of our journey also came directly from God, the Absolute Supreme.

We who have started walking along the spiritual path are the forerunners. All will eventually run towards the same transcendental Goal. The majority of mankind will not always lag behind. All children of God, even those who are now unconscious and unaspiring, will one day run towards humanity's common Goal. This Goal is the supreme discovery of our Divinity and the constant and perfect manifestation of our everlasting Reality.

Who Are We?

Who are we? We are doubters. We are believers. We are discoverers. We are knowers. We are transformers. We are lovers. We are fulfillers.

We are doubters. We doubt our inner dream. We doubt our outer reality. God says to us, "Attention, you doubters! Do not doubt! Your blue-gold dreams are coming from Me. Your green-red realities are running towards Me."

We are believers. We believe that we are helpless and fruitless. God says to us, "Attention, you believers! Your belief is wrong! You are not helpless and fruitless. My Concern is there for you, to help you all the time. My Compassion cares for you, to make your life fruitful at every moment."

We are discoverers. We have discovered that Truth and Light are far beyond our reach. God says to us, "Attention, you discoverers! Your discoveries are all wrong! I have discovered Truth and Light on your behalf. Truth is what you have. Light is what you are."

We are knowers. We know much about things. We know little about ourselves. We know least about God. God says to us, "Attention, you knowers! You know that it is I who have created all things. You know that it is you who create Me every day within you. You know that I am the perfect slave of your constant desires."

We are transformers. We want to transform doubt into belief, fear into strength, bondage into freedom. God says to us, "Attention, you transformers! I am so glad that you want to transform doubt into belief, fear into strength, bondage into freedom. I wish you also to try to transform the life of the finite into the life of the Infinite."

We are lovers. We love beauty's body, beauty's soul and

beauty's goal. God says to us, "Attention, you lovers! Beauty's body is good. Beauty's soul is better. Beauty's goal is by far the best. Beauty's body is an aspiring child. Beauty's soul is the illumining Father. Beauty's goal is the fulfilling Mother."

We are fulfillers. We want to fulfill Heaven on earth, and earth in Heaven. God says to us, "Attention, you fulfillers! You want to fulfill Heaven and earth. It is a splendid ideal. But I wish to say that until you have fulfilled Me, you cannot fulfill Heaven and earth. In order to fulfill Me, you have to cry in your heart ceaselessly and soar above smilingly and everlastingly."

We say to God, "O Father, O Mother, O Friend Eternal, we see that we started our journey as doubters and we shall end our journey as fulfillers."

God says to us, "My sweet children, you are mistaken. You started your journey as the distributors of My Light and My Life-Force, and you will complete your journey as the builders of My Body-Consciousness on earth."

Why Do We Think of God?

Why do we think of God? Why do we pray to God? Why do we meditate on God?

We may think of God, pray to God and meditate on God because the world around us has disappointed us or failed us. Perhaps our near and dear ones have deserted us and therefore we need consolation. If these are the reasons why we think of God, pray to God and meditate on God, then God gives us a mark of 50 out of 100.

We may think of God, pray to God and meditate on God because we feel that we have made thousands of mistakes in this life. We either want to rectify these mistakes or at least not make any more mistakes, since each mistake undoubtedly creates pain and a sense of frustration and failure within us. Again, we may think of God, pray to God and meditate on God because we have missed countless opportunities in life and we want to avail ourselves of all the opportunities that we are going to get in the future. If we think of God, pray to God and meditate on God for these reasons, then God gives us a mark of 60 out of 100.

We may think of God, pray to God and meditate on God because we feel a tremendous sense of fear and doubt in ourselves. We fear the world; we fear even ourselves. We do not know what to say to people or how to behave; we do not know what is going to happen to us. We are always afraid of others or afraid of our own actions. Also, we doubt others and we doubt our own potentialities, possibilities and capacities. For these reasons if we think of God, pray to God and meditate on God, God gives us a mark of 70 out of 100.

We may pray to God for more love in the world and for peace of mind. We do not want to remain in anxiety; we do not want to remain in anger and hatred. If we think of God, pray to God and meditate on God for these reasons, then God gives us a mark of 80 out of 100.

We may think of God, pray to God and meditate on God because we want divine Love and divine Concern from God. We want only the love that will expand us, the love that will fulfill us. We do not expect any outer success or fame or popularity. We wish to receive only God's divine Love. If we think of God, pray to God and meditate on God for these reasons, then God gives us a mark of 90 out of 100.

Finally, we may think of God, pray to God and meditate on God because we want only to become what God is, by virtue of our constant and unconditional self-giving. At this point we are not asking God for anything, nor do we want anything from the world. We want only to be what God is: that is to say, infinite Peace, infinite Light and infinite Bliss. If the world disappoints us, misunderstands us or tortures us, that is up to the world. We do not expect anything from the world, but we do expect one thing from ourselves, and that is to grow into God Himself. If that is our choice, if that is the reason why we think of God, pray to God and meditate on God, then God gives us a mark of 100 out of 100. Otherwise, no matter how sincere our motive is, we will not satisfy God fully. If we want to improve the world or improve ourselves, these goals all have value, but they do not have the ultimate value. The ultimate value we attain only when we are ready and eager to grow into God and become what God is.

How can we grow into God? We must be ready every day to change and to not remain prisoners of the past. When today is over, we have to feel that it is past. It will not be of any help to us in growing into the Highest Supreme. No matter how sweet, how loving, how fulfilling was the past, it cannot give us anything now that we do not already have. We are moving forward towards the goal, and no matter how satisfying the past was, we have to feel that it is now only a prison. The seed grows into a plant and then it becomes a huge tree. If the seed remains a seed, then there will be no further manifestation.

True, we shall remain grateful to the seed because it enabled the plant to grow. But we shall no longer pay much attention to the seed stage. Similarly, once we have become a plant in our life of aspiration, let our aim be to become a tree. Always we have to look forward towards the ultimate Goal. Only when we become the tallest tree will our full satisfaction dawn.

We must always remain in the present. The present is constantly ready to bring the golden future into our heart. Today's achievement is most satisfactory, but we have to feel that today's achievement is nothing in comparison to what tomorrow's achievement will be. Each time satisfaction dawns, we have to feel that this satisfaction is nothing in comparison to the new satisfaction that is about to dawn. We have to feel that every second brings new life, new growth, new opportunity. If we are ready to allow change into our life every second, every minute, every day, we are bound to grow. How will we know that this change is for the better and not for the worse? We will know it is for the better if we see that new light is entering into us. If new light is not entering into us, then we have to feel that we are doing something wrong or making some mistake, unconsciously if not consciously.

Every time we think of God, we should feel that He is our Ideal. He is our Goal. At the same time, we have to know that to see the Goal is not our aim, and even to reach the Goal is not our aim. Our aim is to become the Goal itself. God expects nothing short of this from us. He wants us to be what He is. If this is our aim, then when we think of God, when we pray to God, when we meditate on God, God feels that our thought, our prayer and our meditation are absolutely right, absolutely divine.

The Inner Way

The inner way is the manifestation of the inner creation. The inner creation is the revelation of the inner realization. The inner realization is the dynamic expression of the inner will.

Will is power. Realization is peace. Creation is bliss. Will tells me what I can divinely do for God and for humanity. Realization tells me what God unconditionally does for me and for humanity. Creation tells me what humanity and I can devotedly do for God.

The inner way is the origin of the divine intuition. Intuition carries us to revelation. Revelation shows us the real in the ideal, and the ideal in the real. Intuition is the certainty of Divinity. Divinity is the certainty of Immortality. Immortality is the certainty of Reality.

Divinity's child is man. Immortality's child is the soul. Reality's child is Light.

There are two ways: the inner and the outer. To discover the outer way we need outer power, the power of the body vital and mind. To discover the inner way, we need inner power, the power of the soul.

The outer way always has limited vision. The inner way has the everlasting and ever-transcending Vision. The vision of the outer way culminates in the fast-approaching tomorrow. The vision of the inner way, which marches along the road of Infinity, Eternity and Immortality, has no journey's end. Constantly, spontaneously and soulfully it is marching towards the ever-transcending and ever-fulfilling Beyond.

Idea and Ideal:
The Real and the Eternal

Idea is man's preparation. Ideal is man's progression. The Real is man's illumination. The Eternal is man's realization.

Idea is in the mind. Ideal is in the central being. The Real is in the life of existence. The Eternal is in the soul.

Idea imagines the Truth. Ideal gets a glimpse of the Truth. The Real possesses the Truth. The Eternal is the Truth.

The idea of an unaspiring man is weak, very weak. His ideal is low, very low. His reality is obscure, quite obscure. His Eternity is uncertain, quite uncertain.

The idea of an aspiring man is strong, very strong. His ideal is high, very high. His reality is clear, quite clear. His Eternity is certain, quite certain. His idea is as strong as a giant. His ideal is as high as Mount Everest. His reality is as clear as daylight. His Eternity is as certain as his present divine breath.

An idea knows how to rush forward. An ideal knows how to soar above. The Real knows how to evolve without, from within. The Eternal knows how to glow in the finite and in the Infinite.

Idea tells us, "Awake, arise! You have slept for a long time. It is high time for you to get up." Ideal tells us, "Go and wash yourself, purify yourself. Get ready to study." The Real tells us, "Cultivate your inner life. Discover the Divine within you, the Immortal within you, the Infinite within you." Finally, the Eternal tells us, "I have a short message for you, my children. You have come from me, the ever-unknowable, and you are for me. The unknowable in me you will transform into the unknown; the unknown in me you will transform into the knowable; and the knowable in me you will transform into the known for the earth-aspiration and earth-consciousness."

The Divine Mission

The divine mission is not a self-imposition or a world-proposition. The divine mission is at once love-offering and self-giving.

The world needs attention. The divine mission is always willing to offer its one-pointed attention to the world. The world needs concern. The divine mission is always ready to offer its soulful, meaningful and fruitful concern to the world. The world needs love. The divine mission is always ready to offer its love, inner and outer, to the world. The outer love is constant sacrifice. The inner love is inseparable oneness.

There are two types of seekers: the human seeker and the divine seeker. The human seeker wants to add to his glory, increase his possessions and gain supremacy over others. The divine seeker wants to enter into a spiritual process, a divine progress and a supreme success.

There are two types of nations: the unaspiring nation and the aspiring nation. The unaspiring nation enjoys sleep, ignorance and death. The aspiring nation enjoys self-protection, self-illumination and self-perfection. The unaspiring nation does not know what the Goal is or where the Goal is. The aspiring nation knows what the Goal is and where the Goal is. The Goal is perfect Perfection. The Goal can be found in self-discovery.

There are two types of religions: the unaspiring religion and the aspiring religion. The mission of an unaspiring religion is arrogantly to exclude or find fault with all other religions. The mission of an aspiring religion is to proclaim once and for all that Truth is universal, Light is omnipresent and Love is omnipotent.

There are three significant roads that lead us to our

destination and then make us aware of our divine mission. One road is the road of knowledge and wisdom. The second road is the road of love and devotion. The third road is the road of dedicated action.

If we want to discover our mission while walking along the road of knowledge and wisdom, then we will come to learn *who* God is and *what* God is. We will learn that God is all Love and all Compassion.

If we want to discover our mission while walking along the road of love and devotion, then we will feel *where* God is. God is in our living and flaming faith.

If we want to discover our mission while walking along the path of dedicated action, then we will discover the truth that in revealing our selfless capacity, which is dedication, we are manifesting God's Action on earth.

A spiritual master comes into the world with a mission. His mission is to tell the world that he is *of* God's Illumination but always *for* man's aspiration. Sri Krishna came into the world with a mission, and his mission was the manifestation of universal harmony. The Buddha came into the world with a mission, and his mission was the manifestation of universal peace. The Christ came into the world with a mission, and his mission was the manifestation of universal compassion.

Here at the United Nations, there are many missions representing different countries. Each mission is like a river flowing into the ocean, and the ocean is the United Nations. Each mission is a flowing river entering into the ocean with hope, with eagerness and with the willingness to become part and parcel of the ocean. At the United Nations the divine mission flows not only in the ocean itself, but also through each of the rivers. The divine mission exists not only in the infinite Vast, but also in the tiniest drop of consciousness. In the perfection and fulfillment of the divine mission in the Infinite, and in the perfection and fulfillment of the divine mission in the finite, the supreme satisfaction will dawn. In each of the rivers the supreme satisfaction has to dawn, for it is the constant flow of the rivers entering into the ocean that makes the ocean a living reality. Again, when the ocean flows back into the rivers, it offers them its abundant inner wealth for their fulfillment.

The Mission of God in each permanent mission to the United Nations is as important as it is in the United Nations itself. The United Nations is the body and each mission is like a limb. The body is perfect only when all the limbs are perfect. If one limb is imperfect, the body remains imperfect.

Those who are really great care for the small, the poor, the weak. The mission of the great is to become one with those who are less great than they and to lift them up to a higher standard through self-giving. The mission of those who are not yet great is to feel that the great are only the more evolved extensions of their own aspiring consciousness.

You or I?

O God, are You responsible for all the suffering, darkness and ignorance in the world, or am I?

"Son, I am responsible. I am responsible for everything; I am responsible for everyone; I am responsible for My entire creation. It is I who reside in everything as inspiration and as aspiration. It is I who approve of everything or tolerate everything, show compassion for everything or forgive everything. Therefore, it is I who am responsible for everything, whether it is good or bad, divine or undivine. I am responsible in everything, in every action, in every human life."

O God, You want to change the face of the world. Do You want to do it alone, all by Yourself, or do You need my help and dedicated service?

"Son, I do not want to change the face of the world all by Myself. I cannot change the face of the world alone. I need your assistance. I am the tree. You and all your fellow human beings are the leaves, flowers and fruits. A tree without leaves, flowers and fruits is worthless. I need assistance from my created human beings. I am the ultimate Realization of your climbing cry. You are the ultimate manifestation of My descending Dream. The transformation of the earth-consciousness can take place only when you and I work together. Dedicated service from both the Creator and the creation is needed to change the face of the world."

<hr>

When I think of the divine within my heart, when I meditate on the divine within my heart, I see and feel my real "I". This "I" is not a self-centered "I". This "I" is the infinite expansion of my universal oneness.

When I think of the undivine within my being, when I meditate on the undivine within my being, I automatically choose the life of bondage. I become the life of frustration. I become the life of destruction. When I meditate on the undivine or think of the undivine, I choose mental limitation to be my own. I choose vital frustration to accept me as its own. I choose physical imperfection and inconscience to take me as their very own. Each moment that I meditate on the undivine, I consciously enjoy despair, frustration, limitation, bondage and death.

Here at the United Nations let us say "You and I," not "You or I."

You as a nation—an aspiring nation, a searching nation, a crying nation, an illumining nation—can fulfill the Dream of God on earth. As a seeker of the highest Truth, with your dedication you can fulfill the Dream of God.

When, as a nation, you think only of yourself, I see you as a petal of a rose. But when, on the strength of your dedication to the world at large, you need the Divine in you to think of you and to meditate on you, I see you as a rose, complete and whole. I do not see you as only a petal, but as a fully blossomed rose.

The Divine within us gets abundant joy when we act devotedly and soulfully. The undivine in us gets joy when we want to possess the world and be possessed by the world. We know the secret of joy. When we do the right thing, on the strength of our inner cry, we get joy. But the supreme joy cannot and will not be ours unless and until we know how to devote ourselves. The result of our actions may be satisfactory to us, but if we do not attain this result by virtue of our devoted and selfless service, we will not get infinite Joy, supreme Joy.

Our dynamic joy constantly pleases God.
Our inner silence constantly feeds God.
Our total and integral surrender devours God.

Each action of ours affects the world at large. A state of mind can affect the entire being. An individual can affect the entire humanity. Again, an iota of God's Concern can illumine all of mankind.

> Joy is in self-transcendence.
> Joy is in self-offering.
> Joy is in self-fulfillment.

Each individual knows that when he was in the animal world, he got joy in struggling and fighting. He knows that in the human world, he gets joy, real joy, abiding joy, in serving and in self-giving. He knows that in the future, in his life divine, he will get joy only in becoming his own transcendental Self, which embodies the Light, the Wisdom and the Perfection of the Supreme.

"You or I?" Each individual, when he separates a portion of himself from his entire existence, feels his *you*-consciousness. When an individual uses his hands, if he thinks that his hands are the only reality and not his feet, his head or any other part of himself, then he will hear the song of *you*. But if, while using his hands, he thinks that there will be many occasions when he has to use his legs and other parts of his body, and that therefore all his limbs and organs are important, then there can be no *you* in his existence; it is all *I*.

When we meditate on the Absolute Supreme within us, we clearly see how fruitfully *you* and *I* can work together. We use our legs to go to the office, then we use our hands to work and our head to think. Everything has its own place; everything has its own hour. Each individual has to heed the inner hour and give due importance to everything according to God's Will.

⚬

God, when am I going to know that You and Your entire creation are one?

"The hour has already struck for you to know that I and My

creation are one. If you want to achieve joy or grow into joy by separating Me from My creation, I will have no objection. But you will have only limited joy, limited achievement. If you unite both Me and My creation and take us as one, your joy becomes infinite and your achievement become infinite."

❦

"You or I?" cannot solve the age-long problem of humanity. This problem is the sea of ignorance within us and without. But "you and I" can solve this problem. When the unlit consciousness and the illumined consciousness within us become one, that marks the end of "you or I." At that time we become all oneness, universal oneness: the song of universal oneness, the life of universal oneness and the breath of universal oneness.

How Secure Are We?

When we live in the body, we are constantly insecure. When we live in the vital, we are hopelessly insecure. When we live in the mind, we are surprisingly insecure. When we live in the heart, we are occasionally insecure. When we live in the soul, we are divinely secure. Finally, when we live in God, we are divinely, supremely and sempiternally secure.

What is security? Security is the endless smile of our inner self-confidence. What is self-confidence? Self-confidence is our infinite achievement in the gradual process of our self-transcendence.

In our outer life, we notice two deplorable things: insecurity and impurity. These two defects loom large in our day-to-day life. Insecurity is of ignorance and for ignorance. Impurity is of darkness and for darkness. Likewise, in our inner life, two divine qualities loom large: security and purity. Security is of Light and for Light. Purity is of Bliss and for Bliss.

How insecure are we? If we can offer an adequate answer to this question, then automatically we are running towards our eternal security. How insecure are we? We are extremely insecure. Why are we insecure? We are insecure precisely because we do not claim vastness as our birthright. We are insecure because we do not claim oneness as our soul-right. In our outer life, the power of ignorance wants to offer us its security, which is nothing short of absurdity. In our inner life, the power of Light wants to offer us its security, which is nothing short of complete fulfillment. It is only the power of Light that can offer us satisfaction and perfection.

Security does not lie in our material achievements. Security does not lie in our earthly possessions. The richest man on earth is not secure. His constant anxiety about maintaining and increasing his wealth makes him more insecure than the poorest man on earth. A king, a president or a dictator is not secure. His hunger for sovereign power in ever-increasing measure and his fear of losing the power he has do not allow him to be secure. He is more insecure than the most insignificant human being on earth.

As an individual cannot be secure by amassing material wealth or by attaining heights of power, so a nation cannot be secure by displaying geographical boundaries or by declaring historical achievements. Money-power is no security. Expansion-power is no security. Possession-power is no security. It is the soul-power that is all security. Our love-power, which has free access to the soul-power, is always at our disposal.

Man is a creator and an inventor. He has invented the atom bomb, a destructive power which annihilates all human security. In this case it seems that the creation has more power than the creator. Once the creation emerges from the creator, the creation may threaten the creator himself. But if the inner being of the creator is surcharged with light, then the creator always remains omnipotent. He will not be at the mercy of his creation. Man's inner wisdom-light is infinitely superior to his creation. It is the express will of the creator that the creation will have to execute.

Who created man? God. God's superior Power is oneness. This oneness, inseparable oneness, we can achieve, grow into and become only on the strength of our love. Love is oneness. Oneness is the universal life. Self-giving is God-becoming. Only in God-becoming do we become all security.

Problems

Problems do not indicate man's incapacity. Problems do not indicate man's inadequacy. Problems do not indicate man's insufficiency. Problems indicate man's conscious need for self-transcendence in the inner world, and his conscious need for self-perfection in the outer world.

You have a problem. He has a problem. She has a problem. Your problem is that the world does not touch your feet. His problem is that the world does not love him. Her problem is that she feels she does not adequately help God in the world. To solve your problem, you have to conquer your pride. To solve his problem, he has to conquer his greed. To solve her problem, she has to conquer her self-styled and self-aggrandized desiring ego.

Each problem is a force. But when we see the problem with our inner vision, we feel deep within us a greater force. And when we face the problem, we prove to the problem that not only do we *have* the greatest force, but actually we *are* the greatest force on earth.

A problem increases when the heart hesitates and the mind calculates. A problem decreases when the heart braves the problem and the mind supports the heart. A problem diminishes when the mind uses its searching light and the heart uses its illumining light.

Self-denial cannot solve any problem. Self-assertion cannot solve any problem. It is God-manifestation through our human existence that can solve all problems of the present and the future. Our sincere approach to a problem will eventually lead us to a satisfactory solution. If our approach to God is sincere, He will carry our teeming problems in His Will-Chariot into the infinite, eternal Smile.

If fear is our problem, then we have to feel that we are the chosen soldiers of God the Almighty. If doubt is our problem, then we have to feel that we have deep within us the sea of God's Light. If jealousy is our problem, then we have to feel that we are the oneness of God's Light and Truth. If insecurity is our problem, then we have to feel that God is nothing and can be nothing other than His constant and ceaseless assurance that He will claim us as His very own. If the body is the problem, our constant alertness and attention can solve this problem. If the vital is the problem, our imagination can solve this problem. If the mind is the problem, our illumining inspiration can solve this problem. If the heart is the problem, our perfecting aspiration can solve this problem. If life is the problem, our fulfilling self-discovery can solve this problem.

The individual problem arises when we want to possess the infinite humanity. The universal problem arises when the Infinite wants to mold, guide, shape, transform and divinely and supremely fulfill the finite, but the finite does not want to listen to the dictates of the Infinite.

A problem is not the harbinger of defeat or failure. A problem can be transformed into the beckoning Hands of the Supreme, which can take us to our destined Goal, the Goal of the ever-transcending, ever-fulfilling Beyond.

Beyond the World of Reason

The world of reason is self-partition, self-assertion and self-glorification. Beyond the world of reason is the world of love-realization, oneness-manifestation and God-Perfection.

In the world of reason, the reasoning mind ignores the inner Light and ridicules the higher Light. Beyond the world of reason, the surrendering heart wants to unite itself with the higher Light and the inner Light for the radical transformation of the earth-consciousness.

Here on earth there are three types of satisfaction: the animal satisfaction, the human satisfaction and the divine satisfaction. The animal and the human satisfaction are far, far below the divine satisfaction. A sincere, genuine seeker of the ultimate Truth must go far beyond the world of reason to see the face of supreme satisfaction and to feel the heart of supreme satisfaction.

The animal in us wants to destroy the world for its satisfaction. The human in us wants to govern the world for its satisfaction. The divine us wants to love and serve the world for its satisfaction.

There are two types of mind: the human or physical mind and the spiritual mind. The physical mind is enmeshed in the gross physical consciousness; therefore, it does not and cannot see the proper truth in its own world. The spiritual mind, which is the illumined or illumining mind, has the capacity to stay in the aspiring heart; therefore, it sees the higher Truth, the Truth of the ever-transcending Beyond, and aspires to grow into this Truth.

The human mind does not like to remain in the aggressive and destructive vital consciousness. Yet this human mind, this physical mind, is afraid of the infinite Vast. It wants to achieve the vastness of the Infinite, but at the same time it is afraid of the Infinite. The human mind cares for aesthetic beauty, for poise and balance. The human mind is searching for Truth, for Light, for Reality. But unfortunately, it wants to see the highest Truth in its own limited way. Also, the physical mind wants to examine the highest Truth, which is absurd. It does not want to transcend itself in order to reach the ultimate Truth.

The aspiring inner heart, the psychic heart, knows what it is and what it stands for. It knows that its ultimate realization lies only in its inseparable identification and oneness with Infinity. The heart knows that, even though it is like a tiny drop, when it enters into the mighty ocean of Infinity, it will not lose its identity and personality. On the contrary, its personality and individuality will increase in boundless measure and it will be able to claim the vastness of the sea as its very own. The spiritual mind gets illumination from the soul with the help of the heart. In the process of its own inner illumination, it wants to go far, far beyond the domain of reason in order to see, feel and grow into the ultimate, transcendental Truth.

The paramount importance of the human mind has, until now, been undeniable. The human mind separated us from the animal kingdom through the process of cosmic evolution. Had there been no awakening of the human mind, the conscious human life could not have blossomed out of the animal kingdom. But now the animal in us has played its role. The human in us, the unaspiring human in us, will complete its role soon. The divine in us has now begun its role, or will soon begin.

The soul, the representative of God on earth, will not be satisfied unless and until all the members of its immediate family—the body, the vital, the mind and the heart—march together towards the same goal. The body will serve the Inner Pilot with its dedicated service. The vital will serve the Inner Pilot with its spontaneous determination. The mind will serve the Inner Pilot with its constant search for the Truth-Light of the Beyond. The heart will serve the Inner Pilot with its total and inseparable oneness with the Inner Pilot. When this occurs, all the members of the soul's family will reach their destination, the destination of perfect Perfection on earth.

The transformation of the physical, the transformation of the vital, the transformation of the mind and the transformation of the heart are taking place every day, every hour, every second in each human being. But when a human being consciously aspires, his transformation is quick, convincing and, at the same time, most fulfilling. Therefore, those who pray and meditate are in the world of supreme Truth, Light and Delight. In this world, far, far beyond the domain of the physical mind, we perfectly sing the song of supreme Perfection. Again, we can bring the world of Perfection down into our aspiring and glowing heart through our regular, sincere and devoted surrender to the ultimate Truth.

At the end of our journey, we will see that the animal in us has been transformed and the human in us perfected. We will see that the divine in us has safely and perfectly carried the quintessence of our animal and human life and placed it at the Feet of the Supreme. At that time we can become, here on earth, the direct representatives of the Truth, Light and Delight of the Beyond.

Beyond the world of reason, the Light that we see, feel and aspire to grow into is the Light of illumination. This Light does not want to expose our earthly limitations and deplorable weaknesses. The Upanishads mention that there, in the world beyond reason, the sun shines not. This does not mean that this realm is full of darkness and chaos. There the star-sun shines not, because that world is self-effulgent. There the perfection of the inner Light, the highest Light, the transcendental Light reigns supreme. Seekers of the ultimate Truth eventually enter into that world, the world of transcendental Bliss. When a seeker can establish a free access to that particular world, his heart sings the glory of that world's supreme secret:

"No mind, no form. I only exist."

This "I" is not the earthbound "I", the ego. This "I" is the universal Self, which is birthless and deathless. This is the "I" that comes to the fore when the Divine Lover in us realizes the Supreme Beloved.

In this world, far beyond the domain of reason, God's Vision and God's Reality together live. God's Vision is the cosmic seed, and God's Reality is the universal tree.

The Past, the Present
and the Future

The past is important. The future is more important. The present is most important. The present is infinitely more important than the past and the future put together.

The past is a promise, an unfulfilled promise. The future is a hope, an uncertain hope. The present is necessity's reality and reality's necessity. The present is the Eternal Now. The Eternal is God the Name. The Now is God the Form. When God the Form enters into God the Name, God the Form becomes the transcendental Vision. When God the Name enters into God the Form, God the Name becomes the universal Reality.

Transcendence and immanence, vision and reality are inseparable and invaluable. When we want to become members of the world of vision-dream, transcendence is invaluable. When we want to become members of the world of reality-manifestation, immanence is invaluable.

Transcendence is the seed. Immanence is the fruit. A seed is no seed if it does not reveal the fruit. A fruit is no fruit if it does not embody the seed. The seed and the fruit are at once inseparable and invaluable. In Heaven we are all seeds of God's Dream. On earth we are all fruits of God's Reality.

Education

From the spiritual point of view, what is education? Education is a sacred opportunity to learn and unlearn. What do we learn? We learn God-knowledge. What do we unlearn? We unlearn the teachings of ignorance-night. What is God-knowledge? God-knowledge is self-giving. And what is ignorance-night? Ignorance-night is self-binding.

Education is also a sacred opportunity to achieve. What do we achieve? At the end of our journey's close, we achieve God-perfection. And what is God-perfection? God-perfection is the realization that "I am; I eternally am; I universally am."

Education is continuous self-transcendence. This self-transcendence is not a visionary idea. It is not a chimerical mist. It is not a song for tomorrow's dawn. No! Self-transcendence is a divine reality, an all-fulfilling reality in the immediacy of today.

Education human and education divine. Human education is either an unconscious or a conscious desire to gain supremacy and autocracy. Divine education is our devoted willingness to love and serve the Divine in the human, the Infinite in the finite and the Heaven-free Reality in the earth-bound reality.

Human education, even when it reaches the ultimate rung of the ladder, quite often can be partial, hurtful, aggressive, unlit, obscure, impure and undivine in the truest sense of these terms.

Divine education is spontaneous, soulful and fruitful. It is an inner urge to perfect our outer life and bring to the fore the forgotten essence of Eternity, Infinity and Immortality within us.

Human education, at its very best, is greatness. But this greatness quite often fails to mix with goodness. Therefore, we can safely and unmistakably say that human greatness is blind to goodness. But divine education is goodness within, goodness without.

Again, we have to know that there is human goodness and divine goodness. Human goodness is charity-flower and philanthropy-fruit, which satisfy the human in us. Divine goodness is devotion-flower and surrender-fruit, which satisfy the divine in us and please the Inner Pilot, the Ultimate Absolute within us.

Human education always means money-power and time-power. Divine education is devoted willingness, which far transcends money-power and time-power. Divine education is something that establishes its inseparable oneness with something beyond time and space, far beyond the domain of material power, earthly possessions and earthly achievements.

It is our mother who gives us our education first and foremost. Sri Ramakrishna, the great Indian spiritual Master of Himalayan height, taught us to see each woman as the direct representative of the Divine Mother. It is from our mother that we get not only our first lesson, but also our transcendental lesson. When we see the light of day she tells us, "Children, look around! The earth is beautiful." As years advance upon us, our mother tells us, "Children, dive deep within! There is something which is infinitely more beautiful than the earth." Her final teaching is this: "Children, the beauty of earth and the beauty of Heaven have only one Source, and that Source is God, our Eternity's Beloved Supreme, who is All-Beauty."

From earth we get one kind of education; from Heaven we get another kind of education. We need education both from earth and from Heaven. Thousands of years ago the Vedic Seers offered us a lofty message. Their message was to accept both knowledge and ignorance as one and then finally, to transcend both ignorance and knowledge. They proclaimed:

> He who knows and understands knowledge and igno-
> rance as one, through ignorance passes beyond the
> domain of death, through knowledge attains to an eter-
> nal Life and drinks deep the Light of Immortality.

Through earth-knowledge we make scientific discoveries and become the masters of our earth-life. Through Heaven-wisdom we learn universal love and the feeling of inseparable oneness; we become the lords of our inner existence.

As You See Yourself

Every day, early in the morning, stand in front of a mirror. If you dare to stand in front of a mirror, then you can easily stand in front of the whole world. When you stand in front of the mirror, if you see an undivine face looking back at you, then rest assured that the whole world is undivine. But if you are getting joy from your face, if it is pure and divine, then rest assured that the world is also pure and divine. According to the way you see yourself, the rest of the world will present itself to you. If you see aspiration in your face, I assure you this aspiration you are bound to notice in the whole world. If you see aggressive forces, a devouring tiger inside you, then when you leave the house a big tiger will come and devour you.

We are exact prototypes of the world. We are the microcosm and the world is the macrocosm. A saint always sees everyone in the world—even the worst possible thief—as a saint. Similarly, a thief will see even the most divine saint as a thief. We judge others according to our own standard, according to our own realization. Those who have not realized God will always suspect and doubt those who have. Everyone has to judge others according to his own standard of realization.

Action

Let us not think before we act, for each thought is a heavy burden, a heavy pressure on our shoulders. This burden and this pressure weaken our life-energy considerably.

Let us silence the mind before we act. If we know the art of silencing the mind, not only can we accomplish our tasks faster, but we can do hundreds of things at the same time in a fleeting minute.

Let us not talk before we act, for talk does nothing but bind us to action. We have to be free within and without so that with each action, we can breathe in the fresh air of perfecting, perfected and perfect action.

Let us pray before we act. Each prayer is our soulful devotion, and this devotion is our self-illumining life in action.

Let us not decide before we act. Each decision will be challenged and will be devoured by hesitation. Let us act spontaneously, for each spontaneous action is the expression of our expanding consciousness, the result of our heart's preconceived ideals, the result of our life's preconceived light and the result of our soul's preconceived goal. Action is perfect when it is of God-inspiration and for God-manifestation.

Each desire-action makes us feel how weak, how ignorant, how hopeless, how helpless and how useless we are. Each aspiration-action makes us feel how strong, how powerful, how soulful, how meaningful and how fruitful we are. Again, action for action's sake is not and cannot be the right thing. Action has to be for God's sake.

Before the birth of action, inspiration is our guide. During the course of action, aspiration is our guide. At the end of action, our surrendering height and surrendered depth are our satisfaction and God's Satisfaction.

Inspiration tells action, "Run forward, dive deep within, fly above." Aspiration tells action, "God-Height has not to remain and cannot remain always a far cry." God-Height is our birthright; it is within us. We have only to discover it. When we discover it, we feel that not only does God-Height belong to us, but we belong to it.

Perfection-satisfaction tells us that each individual is not only a direct representative of God on earth, but God Himself in the process of making and shaping His own Vision-Reality yet to be totally fulfilled and His own Reality-Vision yet to be fully manifested.

Each action is God's Song here on earth for God-manifestation, and there in Heaven for God-satisfaction. Each action on earth is God's Dance for humanity's eternal progress and eternal self-transcendence. Each action in Heaven is God's Satisfaction in divinity's self-awakening and self-illumination for a new universe. Each action in Heaven is a new creation and the constant fulfillment of an ever-growing, ever-glowing, ever-satisfying and ever-satisfied God.

Human Art, Divine Art, Supreme Art

First see it and then do it: this is human art. First feel it and then do it: this is divine art. First do it and then become it: this is supreme art.

First see it and then draw it: this is human art. First feel it and then draw it: this is divine art. First live in the inner world with your capacity-light and then live for the outer world's necessity-life: this is supreme art.

Calculation of earth's beauty is human art. Liberation of earth's beauty is divine art. Perfection of earth's beauty is supreme art.

Human art declares, "Nothing succeeds like success." Divine art affirms, "Nothing proceeds like progress." Supreme art whispers, "Nothing satisfies like service, divine service, soulful service."

The lofty height of human art is the inspiration-moon. The sublime depth of divine art is the aspiration-sun. The illumining goal of supreme art is Eternity's perfection-day.

Beauty's possession is earth's art. Beauty's distribution is Heaven's art. Beauty's satisfaction is supreme art.

Earth's appreciation of beauty is earth's art. Heaven's compassion for beauty is Heaven's art. God's Perfection in beauty is supreme art.

Human art looks around while running towards the goal. Divine art looks ahead while running fast, faster, fastest towards the goal. Supreme art does not run, does not fly, does not dive. Supreme art becomes what the Inner Pilot, the Supreme Artist, wants it to become.

Human art is the reality that we have, the reality that needs expression, the reality that needs world-acceptance, world-appreciation, world-admiration, world-adoration. Divine art is the divinity that we see in the inner world and the outer world, in the world of our earthly experiences, earthly realizations, earthly sacrifices and earthly achievements. Supreme art is the divine reality that is constantly transcending its own height for God's ever-new creation, ever-new revelation, ever-new manifestation and ever-new perfection.

Human art is the leaf-experience of our life-tree. Divine art is the flower-realization of our life-tree. Supreme art is the fruit-perfection of our life-tree.

A leaf inspires us; therefore, we run towards our destination. A flower purifies us; therefore, our speed becomes tremendous and we run fast, faster, fastest. A fruit energizes us; therefore, we become chosen instruments to fight against teeming darkness and ignorance, to conquer the undivine forces within us and finally, to establish within ourselves the real, the divine, the eternal silence-life and perfection-beauty.

Each creation of God embodies the real reality. This real reality is the soul. The soul of an object cannot be as developed, as illumining, as fulfilling as the soul of an advanced seeker or a realized master. If we want to draw a bench or a chair, we may draw it well, but our inspiration is bound to fail us after a few minutes. But if we draw someone or something that has contributed considerably to the world of aspiration and light, then naturally our inspiration will last a long, long time. In this case, inspiration is the precursor of aspiration, aspiration is the precursor of revelation and revelation is the precursor of manifestation, which is none other than God-perfection: complete, absolute perfection.

The human artist is great, undoubtedly great. The divine artist is good, unmistakably good. The supreme artist is he who cares neither for greatness nor for goodness. The supreme artist longs for only one thing: God-satisfaction, the satisfaction of God the Supreme Artist in and through him.

Punishment

To be on my own side and not on God's side is not only an unpardonable crime, but also an unbearable punishment.

My Lord's punishment-dog cannot change me and my life. It is only the constant increase of my love for my Lord that can and will change me and my human life totally.

The punishment that I get from my Supreme Pilot when I disobey Him is next to nothing in comparison with the punishment that I inflict upon myself by separating myself from my sweetest and closest oneness with Him, in Him and for Him.

When I do something wrong, no matter how trivial and insignificant it is, my Lord Supreme, do punish me immediately: for that is what I richly deserve. But do love me even when You punish me, for Your Love is my aspiration-life's only soul and my dedication-life's only goal.

Success and Progress

Meditation defines success and progress in life. Success is the body-dance of self-gratification. Progress is the heart-song of self-perfection.

Success says, "I am above you. You are below me." Progress says, "I only want to be ahead of myself."

Success is my temporary achievement on earth. Progress is my lasting achievement in God and God's lasting achievement in me.

Success thinks that it needs only confidence and perseverance. Progress thinks that it needs not only confidence and perseverance, but something infinitely more, and that is God's infinite Grace and God the infinite Grace.

The difference between God's infinite Grace and God the infinite Grace is this: God's infinite Grace paves the way for the Hour of God to strike before God grants us what He wants to grant us. But God the infinite Grace not only wants to expedite the Hour, He also does everything unconditionally, in the twinkling of an eye.

Experience is the pioneer-runner of success. Illumination is the pioneer-runner of progress. Success is the measure of man in earth-bound time. Progress is the measure of man in Heaven-free time.

Success fights against teeming opposition and destroys it. Progress fights against teeming opposition, too; but instead of destroying it, progress transforms opposition into perfection for God's greatest Satisfaction in and through man on earth.

Success is an idea well-proclaimed and well-acclaimed. Progress is an ideal well-distributed and well-accepted.

Success is the preserver of today's strong arms. Progress is the preserver of yesterday's searching mind, today's aspiring heart and tomorrow's totally consecrated life.

Success is my promise to humanity's curious eye. Progress is my promise to humanity's loving heart, to divinity's unifying soul and to God's all-sheltering and all-loving Feet.

The Face of Truth

A seeker wishes to see the face of Truth in spirituality, in religion, in love, in brotherhood, in every field of reality, in every branch of the reality-tree. But unfortunately, the face of Truth is not to be found there. The face of Truth is found only in longing, in the longing for Truth. Not only the face of Truth, but the very heart of Truth is to be found only in the longing itself. What is Truth? Truth is the longing, the birthless and deathless longing which we have and which we are. This is the only Truth—nothing more, nothing less.

Some seekers are of the opinion that Truth is not to be found here on earth, that Truth belongs to the hoary past, that it is a memory of the past we are carrying and dragging. But this is not true. Truth was there before, Truth is here now and Truth will always be present in the future.

The Truth of the past is the Truth-beauty in God's cosmic Vision. The Truth of the present is the earth-duty in God's cosmic Realization. The Truth of the future is the Truth-infallibility in God's cosmic Manifestation.

Here on earth, a seeker notices three kinds of Truth: peripheral Truth, median Truth and core Truth.

Peripheral Truth says, "Love is the essence of life, but there is no love on earth."

Median Truth says, "I love mankind. Therefore, it is obligatory on the part of all human beings to love me."

Core Truth, the Truth of the inmost reality, says, "I love God the Creator, for He is none other than Love. I love God the creation, because it is nothing other than love."

Truth needs a possessor, a revealer and a fulfiller. The Truth-possessor is he who is at least a few centuries in advance of his time. The Truth-revealer is he who stands in front of humanity, faces humanity, enters into humanity's countless needs and transforms humanity's needs into deeds. The Truth-fulfiller is he who lives only for humanity, for humanity's sake. Unless and until each human being becomes a perfect instrument of the Absolute Supreme, the task of the Truth-fulfiller is not complete.

A seeker of the highest, ultimate Truth, a seeker who has established his constant oneness with the Absolute, can at once be a Truth-possessor, a Truth-revealer and a Truth-fulfiller. This he can do on the strength of his oneness with the perennial Source, his oneness with the transcendental Light.

We are all seekers, seekers of the United Nations, for the United Nations. The United Nations itself is both the seeker and the Truth. When we look at the body-reality of the United Nations, we see that the United Nations plays the role of the seeker. When we look at the soul-reality of the United Nations, we see that the United Nations is nothing short of Truth, Light and Delight.

The seeker in the United Nations is becoming and growing into the Truth-reality, and the Truth-reality is constantly unveiling its hidden treasures—its immortalizing, all-illumining and all-fulfilling treasures. These treasures are concern, sympathy, union, oneness, justice-light, perfection and finally, satisfaction in all that the United Nations does and all that the United Nations is going to do. The United Nations is growing into the perfection-tree that will offer its branches of concern, sympathy and oneness to humanity.

When we seek, we long for a reality. When we long for a reality which is other than our true self, this reality will always remain a far cry. If we live in the body-reality and from this body-reality try to reach the soul-reality, then we shall never succeed. But if we can dare to say and feel that there is only one reality—the soul-reality—which is founded upon our universal oneness-reality, our transcendental oneness-reality, only then can we safely say that inside our longing itself is the birthless and the deathless Truth. Then we can say that our longing itself is the everlasting Truth, the immortal Truth, the eternally transcending Truth, the infinitely fulfilling Truth.

Truth

Truth is God's Treasure and man's property. Truth is God's eternal and constant Progress and man's energizing success. Truth is God's Natural History and man's supernatural mystery.

Truth is original and essential when it comes from the soul. Truth is pure and sure when it comes from the heart. Truth is obscure and incomplete when it comes from the mind. Truth is undivinely dynamic and imperfect when it comes from the vital. Truth is weak and insignificant when it comes from the body.

The body is blind. The vital is wild. The mind is ignorant. The heart is aspiring. The soul is perfect. Out of His infinite Bounty, God offers His clearing Sight to the body, His embracing Might to the vital, His illumining Light to the mind, His transcending Height to the heart and His fulfilling Right to the soul.

Truth is our inner attitude. Truth is our outer aptitude. Truth is our life's fortitude. When attitude, aptitude and fortitude play together and sing the song of aspiration, Infinitude dawns on them, and soon they bathe in the purest effulgence of Infinitude.

In the world of desire, Truth is our mind's idea. In the world of aspiration, Truth is our heart's ideal. In the world of realization, Truth is our soul's Goal.

Idea is the seed. Ideal is the tree. Goal is the fruit. Idea is self-expression. Ideal is self-expansion. Goal is self-union.

Emotion: Our Foe or Our Friend?

Emotion is both our foe and our friend. There are many planes of consciousness, but usually we deal with two: the physical and the spiritual. On the physical plane, emotion at the very outset is sweet, sweeter, sweetest. Then there comes a time when this emotion is followed by frustration. Finally, frustration is followed by destruction. Why does it happen so? It happens so precisely because the emotion that is in play in the physical proper is still unlit, unillumined and impure. On the physical plane, emotion is nothing short of self-exposition, either consciously or unconsciously, either under compulsion or at one's own sweet will.

There is another kind of emotion on the spiritual plane, in our heart or psychic existence. Here the emotion is constantly self-illumining and God-fulfilling. In the spiritual world, in the inner world, emotion is Truth-expansion, divinity-revelation and perfection-manifestation. Naturally, we can also add God-satisfaction, for God-satisfaction can loom large only in Truth-expansion, divinity-revelation and perfection-manifestation.

On the human plane there are quite a few undivine forces that attack us and eventually compel us to surrender: anxiety, worries, attachment and self-pity.

Anger: what is it, after all? Anger is a force that does not permit us to be consciously aware of our oneness-reality with others, who are our extended, expanded reality. When anger assails us, we not only forget our oneness-reality with others, but we actually destroy our oneness-reality.

How do we conquer anger? If we can make our mind calm and quiet, and pray and meditate on God. Then we will be able to free ourselves from the wild anger in us. But if we want to conquer anger on the spot, then the easiest and the most effective way is to repeat God's Name as fast as possible each time we breathe in. The first time we breathe in, we can repeat God's Name ten times. The second time we breathe in, if each time we say "God" we can mentally visualize God's Name 20 times more, then the power of our anger practically vanishes.

Anger is lack of poise, lack of mental equanimity. How do we attain poise? How do we achieve mental equanimity? We achieve mental equanimity when we live not in the mind but somewhere else. And where is that place? It is in the heart.

The mind that doubts, the mind that is subject to anxiety, worries, suspicion and attachment cannot give us poise. It is the heart, the aspiring heart that has already established its constant and conscious oneness with the soul, that can give us poise, clarity and vision. The poise that we get from the heart can easily be brought into the suspicious, doubtful, arrogant, unlit, unillumined mind. Once the poise of the heart, which is founded upon the soul's light, is brought into the human mind, which is immersed in the gross physical, the mind is bound to be illumined, slowly, steadily and unerringly.

What is poise? Poise is a kind of divine emotion in us. It is anything but excitement. This poise we get when we identify ourselves with the Infinite, the Eternal, the Immortal.

Fear is another emotion which succeeds in separating us from our vast oneness-reality. Doubt does the same. When fear plays its role, we either unconsciously or consciously separate our existence from the Vastness itself. When doubt plays its role, we unconsciously shorten our own reality-existence. We minimize our consciousness, our own experience and our realization of Reality.

Attachment is a form of emotion. When there is attachment, we immediately notice a constant tug-of-war between two armies. Attachment binds us to our own gratification. Attachment makes us feel that no individual is complete. It makes us feel that only in the unification of two individuals— whether it is on the physical plane, the vital plane or the mental plane—will these two individuals derive satisfaction.

But this feeling is incorrect. The human in us is right now half-animal. The animal consciousness in us quite often plays its role most powerfully. Therefore, when two people use attachment as a magnet to pull each other, quite often destruction plays its role.

Detachment is also a form of emotion. On the outer plane, we may feel that there is no emotion involved in detachment. Unfortunately, this conception of ours is not true. Detachment is not indifference. Detachment is our true existence, the existence that lives in reality proper—either in Heaven-reality or in earth-reality. Detachment is emotion, but it is not affected by the happenings, incidents and experiences of the reality that it is seeing; it is always an inch higher in consciousness. Although detachment may remain on the earth plane, in the midst of earth's multifarious activities, it keeps its consciousness higher than the plane where the experiences or incidents are taking place.

Although a true seeker is detached, that does not mean he is indifferent. He sees and experiences the reality that is apt to threaten him and frighten him, the reality that quite often belittles his capacity, his potentiality and even his own existence and immortality. But the seeker does not let this reality affect him. He feels there is only one reality within him, and that reality is God-Reality. This God-Reality he can feel and experience no matter where he is, provided he knows the supreme art of focusing all his attention on one object or subject: God.

Sincerity and insincerity: these are also emotions. With sincerity we fly in the vast, uncharted sky. With insincerity we enter into a tiny cave in order to escape. With sincerity we try to spread our wings and give to the world what we have and what we are. With insincerity we hide our reality-world, which we claim to be ours alone.

Purity and impurity are also emotions. Purity is our self-expansion and impurity is our self-destruction. With each purity-breath we breathe in, we increase our God-Reality. And with each impurity-breath we breathe in, we surrender our very existence to the jaws of death.

Sincerity and purity are the two divine attributes that all seekers can apply to their day-to-day activities. Emotion has to be disciplined sincerely in the mind proper. When the mind becomes sincere, the mind opens itself consciously, devotedly and soulfully to the Vastness. When sincerity dawns in the mind, multifarious encouraging and inspiring experiences of the world descend from Above through the mind and prepare the mind for its universal opening to the transcendental Heights.

Purity is of the heart and in the heart, but for the soul. The soul is the conscious representative of God within us. The heart of purity is the heart that consciously discovers God. The heart of purity is conscious God-revelation and God-manifestation.

Ultimately all our emotions give way to tears, either earthly tears or Heavenly tears. Earthly tears are the outcome of depression, frustration and lack of fulfillment. Heavenly tears are the tears of gratitude offered to the Source, to the Supreme Beloved, the Inner Pilot, the Eternal Friend.

We start our journey with earthly tears because this is what we get when we walk along the road of desire. But there comes a time when we discover that the road we are walking upon will never lead us to our destination. Then we start walking along another road, the road of realization. When we walk along this road, each day, each hour, each minute, each second we feel we are approaching our cherished destination. Then the tears that we experience are divine tears composed of our unalloyed love for God and flowing from our heart-flower of gratitude.

With earthly tears we start our journey. But this journey does not satisfy us; it cannot lead us to our destination. Therefore we resort to Heavenly tears, which come from our heart's gratitude and true love of God. When we actually become our Heavenly tears, we not only start our journey properly but also hasten our true Truth-realization and God-revelation, which is Beauty-revelation, God-manifestation and Bliss-manifestation for earth.

Emotion that says, "I came, I saw, I conquered," is the destructive emotion, the animal emotion in us. Emotion that says, "I came, I loved, I became," is divine emotion, illumined emotion, fulfilled emotion, perfect, all-illumining, all-fulfilling emotion.

"I am for myself" is the message of either the animal emotion in me or the human emotion in me. "I am for my Reality-Source, for my Reality-God" is the message of divine emotion. I see the Truth just because the Truth wants to see in and through me. I become the Truth just because the Truth reveals itself in and through me. Then I am inundated with divine emotion, which is conscious and constant love of God and awareness of God, Truth-expansion, God-manifestation and man and God-satisfaction.

A New Year

A new year means a new experience. The new year experiences a new aspiration from human beings. Aspiration is a climbing cry that becomes an illumining smile.

Human beings expect a new satisfaction from the new year. Satisfaction is the embodiment and manifestation of happiness. When we embody happiness, each little individual world of ours becomes a big and vast world. When we manifest happiness, the mortal in us becomes immortal.

What is happiness? Happiness is what God eternally has and what God supremely is. Happiness is not something inside the heart of self-giving. No! It is our unconditional self-giving itself. Self-giving is God-becoming, slowly in Reality, steadily in Divinity and unerringly in Immortality.

Each new year reminds us of the ideal and the real in us. The ideal in us is to see the Truth. The real in us is to become the Truth. Truth is the Eye of God in Heaven; Truth is the Heart of God on earth. God's Eye guides us and leads us. God's Heart feeds us and immortalizes us.

Each new year is a new responsibility. A new responsibility is a new opportunity. What is the message of opportunity? Opportunity tells us that our ultimate Goal does not have to remain always a far cry. The Goal can be reached by transforming animal hunger into divine hunger. The goal can be reached by transforming human thirst into divine thirst. Animal hunger devours the divine vision in us. Human thirst dominates the divine reality in us. Divine hunger is for self-transcendence. Divine thirst is for self-perfection.

A new year offers the message of either destruction or satisfaction. If we please ourselves in our own human way, then we will undoubtedly meet with destruction. If we please God in God's own Way, then we shall without fail meet with satis-faction. To doubt the divine in us and to indulge the human in us is to please ourselves in our own human way. To per-fect the human in us and to fulfill the divine in us is to please God in God's own Way.

On a Birthday

Each birthday is a new awakening. Each birthday is a new hope. Each birthday is a new promise. Each birthday is a new fulfillment.

The new awakening takes place in our physical, earth-bound consciousness. The new hope dawns in our frustrated, disappointed and unaspiring vital. The new promise comes inside our doubtful human mind. This new promise challenges the doubting, doubtful mind and reminds the mind of its origin: consciousness-flood. The new fulfillment occurs inside the entire being: in the earth-bound being and the Heaven-free being.

When the soul descends to earth, the soul takes responsibility not only for the earth-consciousness, but also for the Heaven-consciousness. The earth-consciousness cries for light, peace, love and delight. The soul promises the earth-consciousness that it will help it achieve peace, light, love, delight, joy, harmony and everything that the earth-consciousness needs. Again, it is the same soul that promises the Heaven-consciousness that it will manifest Heaven's joy, satisfaction and perfection here on earth.

Each birthday is a tune, a melody of the universal music. Each individual is also a melody of the universal music. The seeker grows and glows in his music, which he can hear with his soulful ears. The very presence of the soul-child inside us is what grants us a taste of the universal music. The soul needs to climb like music, soulful music. When it climbs, the soul knows no religious barriers, no political boundaries. It is all freedom within and without.

Each birthday is a petal of a flower. The flower blossoms petal by petal, and then it is ready to be placed at the inner shrine in the aspiring heart.

A divine thought indicates a new birthday. An iota of will indicates a new birthday. An upward movement indicates a new birthday. At every moment, whether we look within or without, we celebrate the birthday of our oneness with God, the Creator of the entire universe. When we look at something, we become one with it. On a birthday we feel our inseparable oneness with the expansion of a new light, a light that will ultimately cover the length and breadth of the world.

The real birthday does not come only once a year. The real birthday is the birth of each second in a seeker's life. An aspiring second in the seeker's heart marks his real birthday. At every moment, God, the Author of all good, celebrates the seeker's birthday.

As seekers, we have to be consciously aware of something divine and supreme within us. This divine and supreme thing is our promise to humanity and our promise to Divinity. The transformation of humanity's face is our soul's promise to humanity. The manifestation of Divinity's Light here on earth is our soul's promise to Divinity.

Courage Versus Humility

Courage challenges the world. Humility illumines the world. Courage strongly urges us to stand up for our own rights. Humility soulfully inspires us to stand up for God's rights alone.

Courage is not aggression. Aggression is man's destruction-force. Humility is not humiliation. Humiliation is man's rejection-force. Courage is man's self-determination. Humility is man's oneness-distribution. Self-determination eventually succeeds. Oneness-distribution constantly proceeds.

Courage is man's conquering force. Humility is man's unifying force. Courage feeds the divine human in us. Humility feeds the unifying and immortal divine in us.

The seeker in us uses courage to conquer our teeming doubts in the mental world. The seeker in us uses humility to constantly increase our faith in God's universal Oneness and Light.

Courage is the struggle, birthless and deathless, between man's victory and defeat, between man's joy and sorrow, between man's smiles and tears, between man's acceptance and rejection, between what man has and what man is. What man has is sound-satisfaction and what man is, is silence-perfection.

Humility is man's divine and supreme glory-bird that flies from God's Infinity-Dawn to God's Eternity-Day and from God's Eternity-Day to God's Infinity-Dawn.

With courage we manifest God in our own way. With humility God manifests Himself in and through us in His own Way.

We Must Not Give Up!

Let us keep going. We must not give up! Although the dragon-thoughts of frustration assail us, we must not give up! There is definitely a goal, and this goal must needs be ours. We must not give up!

Although Heaven does not feed our heart's cry regularly, although earth does not entirely support our spiritual journey, still we must not give up!

Let us invoke the presence of our indomitable courage-fount to help us conquer the feelings of loneliness and unworthiness. We must not give up!

Although the world does not appreciate us, although the world does not see the beauty and the light in us, we must not give up appreciating the world. Indeed, this world of ours is also an instrument of God. Like us, it considers God-realization, God-revelation and God-manifestation as its bounden duty. Therefore, we must appreciate the world. After all, what is appreciation? Appreciation is self-expansion. Self-expansion is oneness-awareness, and oneness-awareness is Truth-distribution. We must not give up!

Although we do not have a sunny present, although we had a foggy past, although we suspect inclement weather in the near future, we must not give up!

With our mind's resolution, our heart's determination and our soul's illumination, we shall eventually succeed in life. Success is our choice. Progress is God's Choice. Man chooses to become. He becomes confidence-lion within and confidence-elephant without. God chooses to give. He gives us His universal Light constantly, unreservedly and unconditionally. He gives us His transcendental Delight constantly, unreservedly and unconditionally.

We must not give up! Let us prepare ourselves for God's choice Hour. We must not give up!

Expectation

Expectation is frustration, especially when I want to possess the world. Expectation is frustration, especially when I want to lord it over the world. Expectation is frustration, especially when I want the world to surrender to my will.

Expectation has its justification when I love the world and want the world to offer me a gratitude-heart. Expectation has its justification when I pray to God for the betterment, for the transformation, for the illumination of the world and want the world to offer me a gratitude-heart. Expectation has its justification when I sincerely, devotedly and unreservedly try to elevate the earth-consciousness according to my capacity and want the world to offer me a gratitude-heart.

Expectation is nothing short of satisfaction when I wait devotedly, soulfully and unconditionally for God's choice Hour to arrive to liberate, illumine, transform, perfect and fulfill me. Expectation is satisfaction when I feel in the inmost recesses of my heart that God is not only my sovereign Lord, the Absolute Supreme, but also my Friend, my eternal Friend and only Friend. Expectation is satisfaction, especially when I know that God has done everything for me in the inner world. This discovery of mine is founded on my faith, my inner faith in Him, not because He has done everything for me, not because He is all Love for me, but because I have realized something else that is infinitely more significant than all this. My realization is this: my God, my Lord Supreme, my eternal Friend, is everything in and through me. He is expanding and enlarging His own cosmic Vision in and through me. When I realize my expectation of what He has done for me and what He is to me, my life has its soulful purpose and fruitful delight.

When I use the human in me to serve any purpose, my expectation becomes frustration. When I use the divine in me to serve any purpose, my expectation has its justification. At that time expectation itself is justification. But when I use my Lord Supreme, my eternal Friend, to fulfill something, my expectation is satisfaction, for the expectation is the Vision-Light, and the satisfaction is the Reality-Delight. They are one and inseparable.

Divine Friends and Undivine Foes

If you are a beginner in the spiritual life, you have to feel that you are standing inside your room behind a closed door. It is up to you to recognize whom to accept as your friends and whom not to accept. Faith, love, devotion, surrender, courage, will-power: these are your friends. You will allow these persons to come into your room, and then you must bolt the door from inside to keep out your enemies. Fear, doubt, anxiety and worry: these are your enemies. If you allow them, they will come into your room most gladly. As a matter of fact, they are always there, waiting to come in, but you do not allow them.

Once your friends have entered your room and you have bolted the door, you can start conversing with your friends. Each time a devoted friend of yours speaks to you, immediately the power or capacity of that friend increases inside you. When your friend who embodies love speaks of love, immediately your love for God increases. You also have a friend who embodies courage. When this friend speaks of inner courage, immediately your own inner courage comes to the fore.

When your surrender-friend speaks to you, you will see that your spiritual surrender becomes easy and spontaneous. Previously you thought that surrender meant self-extinction. You were afraid of surrender because you thought that your individuality would disappear. But when this friend of yours who embodies surrender tells you what divine surrender is, immediately you are eager to throw yourself into the surrender-sea. In this divine surrender you are not losing anything. On the contrary, you are becoming the vast Infinite itself. In this way, when these friends of yours tell you about their own qualities and what these qualities represent on earth, immediately you will make the fastest progress.

A beginner in the spiritual life should always make a careful selection when it is a matter of friendship, for a beginner's progress depends entirely on the friendship he has made with divine or undivine qualities. Establishing a friendship with divine qualities is the easiest and most effective way for a beginner to make the fastest progress. Later, when he becomes advanced, the so-called friends that wanted to enter into him—fear, doubt, anxiety and worry—will feel that it is a hopeless case. Once the seeker is advanced, he will never, never make the mistake of allowing fear, doubt or other undivine elements to enter into him. When the seeker becomes advanced, fear, doubt and other undivine forces come to realize that they are knocking at the wrong door.

Right now if you are a beginner, at any moment doubt can assail you. Doubt may make you feel that doubting is good, but please do not be fooled. If you doubt as much as you can, eventually doubt itself will fail you. Then doubt will send its best friend, the reasoning mind. The reasoning mind will tell you, "All right, doubt has failed you. But if you proceed in this direction, perhaps you will get what you want. If you do not proceed this way, you will not get satisfaction." The reasoning mind will create darkness and confusion. In the spiritual life you will come to know that doubt is only poison and the reasoning mind simply useless. A spiritual person does not reason; he just gives. A beginner especially should always act like a child. When a child comes to his mother, he does not use the reasoning mind. He acts without the mind. He just runs to his mother and gives her everything that he has found on his way, whether it is divine or undivine. He gives to his mother gladly, cheerfully and devotedly what he has, and the mother gives him what she has. Naturally, the mother has infinitely more than the child.

As a sincere seeker, you should allow only the divine forces to enter into you. Each time a divine force operates, you gain or achieve that divine quality in yourself. Gradually all the divine qualities will blossom in you like a flower, petal by petal, slowly, steadily and perfectly. Finally, you will be fully ready to offer yourself at the Feet of the Lord Supreme.

There are some forces that will attack you and there are some that will help you. You must always be on the alert; you have to open your eyes and allow only those forces that will elevate your consciousness to come in. When you become advanced, wrong forces will not dare to come near you. Now they may dare, because you are a beginner; but you will not remain a beginner forever. If you continue walking along the right path, you will become advanced. You are bound to make progress and reach your destined Goal.

Humanity's Promise

Humanity's promise to humanity is a life of service. Humanity's promise to Divinity is a life of oneness. Humanity's promise to God is a life of perfection. Again this perfection is preceded and followed by service and oneness. Oneness has to be found in perfection and service has to be found in oneness. Therefore, we can safely say that humanity's promise to God is a life of service, oneness and perfection.

Service is Eternity's meaningful achievement. Oneness is Infinity's soulful achievement. Perfection is Immortality's fruitful achievement. Service is the transformation of the human within us. Oneness is the realization of the divine within us. Perfection is the satisfaction of the Supreme within us.

God says to the body, "Body, promise Me that you will not always sleep." The body says to God, "Father, I promise You that I shall listen to You. Now, accept a promise of my own. My promise to You is that I shall try to be always wakeful, alert and vigilant."

God says to the vital, "Vital, promise Me that you will no longer be aggressive." The vital says to God, "Father, I shall abide by Your Command. In addition, I wish to offer You a promise of my own. From now on, I shall be divinely dynamic always."

God says to the mind, "Mind, promise Me that you will no longer cherish your friendship with doubt. Doubt can no longer be your friend." The mind says to God, "Father, I shall definitely listen to You. I also have a promise of my own, and that promise is that I shall make friends only with faith. I will have faith only as my friend. I shall live with faith and I shall fulfill my existence on earth only in faith and for faith—soulful, fruitful, all-offering, all-embracing faith."

God says to the heart, "Heart, promise Me that from now on you will not feel insecure under any circumstances." The heart says to God, "Father, I give You my word of honor that I shall not in any way feel insecure. I shall listen to Your Command. My promise to You is that I shall establish my oneness-existence with each human being in Your entire creation. I shall feel and cherish my oneness with all human beings throughout the length and breadth of the world."

The divine in us promises; the human in us forgets. Again, the Supreme in us revives all our countless promises and fulfills them. Our promise and our aspiration—the inner cry, the mounting flame—are two intimate friends. Promise says to aspiration: "Friend, I do know what to do. I have to establish a life of divinity here on earth. Then there will be no ignorance, no darkness, no limitations, no bondage. I know that this is what I have to accomplish." Aspiration says to promise: "Friend, let me tell you how you can do it. You can do it only on the strength of your self-giving. Give what you have and give what you are at every moment. Only then will your Goal not remain a far cry. What do you have? A soulful cry. This is what you can give to mankind. And what are you? You are God's eternal Dream, the Dream that every moment is in the process of blossoming."

Humanity's promise is a movement forward, upward and inward. Humanity's forward movement leads us to the universal Reality and helps us claim the entire creation of God as our very own. Humanity's upward movement carries us to the transcendental Height and helps us claim the transcendental Reality as our very own. Humanity's inward movement leads us to God Himself: God the Dream, God the Reality, God the Silence, God the Sound, God the Omniscient, Omnipotent and Omnipresent. It is within our aspiration's abode that God's Presence looms large.

Our forward movement is for the recognition of the universal Reality. Our upward movement is for the recognition of the transcendental Reality. Our inward movement is for the recognition of the eternally Real in us: God the Supreme.

Humanity has a promise. This promise is self-discovery. Self-discovery comes from self-mastery and self-mastery comes from self-discovery. When we dive deep within, we discover our reality-existence, and when we spread our vision-light around us, we achieve self-mastery. The most effective way to attain self-mastery is to spread our heart's light, which is the Vision of the Supreme within us. If we spread our vision-light, then the darkness around us surrenders and becomes transformed.

Humanity itself is a promise: a promise of God to Himself, for each individual is a portion of God's Reality-Existence and God's Vision-Existence. Each individual is a representative of God's ultimate Height on earth. In and through each individual, God fulfills something unique in Himself. God's Promise to Himself is His Aspiration, His Realization, His Revelation and His Manifestation in and through each individual being.

Each individual has already made an inner promise to humanity. Again, humanity also has made an inner promise to each individual. Each individual, when he prays and meditates and enters into his highest transcendental Height, looks around and sees countless beings around him. At that time he feels it is his bounden duty to carry all and sundry—all human beings, all his brothers and sisters—to the highest Height. This is his promise. And humanity, as a collective soul, promises to each individual that it will offer him the universal Light and Delight. Mere height is not enough. Length and breadth as well as height are equally needed. Vision and reality have to embrace the entire creation. The individual will carry the collective soul to the Height and humanity, the collective soul, will carry the individual to the universal Reality within all of us.

We have to know whether we shall always remain with mere promise or whether we shall go one step ahead. That step is commitment. There is a great difference between promise and commitment. Promise can be a mere word, a meaningless, fruitless and lifeless gift. But when it is a matter of commitment, the soul's commitment to mankind, inside that commitment itself the illumining reality and the fulfilling reality abide.

The promises that we have made to God, to mankind and to ourselves must be transformed into conscious, constant and unconditional commitments. It is inside the heart of commitment that all the promises of the past, present and future can blossom into fulfilling reality. Humanity's promise to God is: "I am offering myself to You. Take me." God's promise to humanity is: "I am accepting you."

Each soul offers a solemn promise to mankind when it enters into the earth-arena. Ordinary souls and special souls both make promises. In the case of ordinary souls, because of countless weaknesses and the teeming ignorance all around, it is difficult for them to fulfill their promises. But great souls quite often fulfill their promises because they have an indomitable will. Souls of the superlative degree, who are constantly one with the Will of the Supreme, who are absolutely direct representatives of the Supreme, come into the world with the loftiest promise. Unlike ordinary souls or even great souls, they deal with the entire humanity. Their promise is most sublime and, at the same time, most difficult to execute. But they are not earth-bound. They are Heaven-free. They live on earth for a few years—30, 40, 50 or 80 years—and then they go back to their Heavenly abode. Three souls of the highest caliber, the highest magnitude, the highest order who have come into the world are Sri Krishna, the Buddha and the Christ. Sri Krishna came into the world to establish the divine code of life: righteousness must reign supreme; wickedness must give way to righteousness and a life of light. His promise has not yet been fulfilled. There are still wicked people on earth; wickedness still looms large and reigns supreme. But Sri Krishna has not given up his promise. In and through you, me and each individual, he is trying to conquer humanity's wickedness and replace it with the divine code of life, which is justice-light all-where.

The Buddha promised to make the world at large a world without suffering. There will not remain an iota of suffering here on earth, he said. He tried his best, but the world is still suffering tremendously. Yet the Buddha has not given up his promise. His promise is now being executed in and through us, in and through each individual seeker here on earth. Each seeker wants to free himself and also the entire world from suffering. In this way, the loftiest promise of the Buddha is now being executed in and through each individual seeker on earth.

Another soul of the highest magnitude is the Christ, the Son, the Savior. His promise to mankind was the establishment of the Kingdom of Heaven. We all know what the Kingdom of Heaven will look like. There will be no ignorance, no darkness, no bondage, no limitation, but only boundless light, boundless delight, boundless harmony, boundless peace. All divine qualities in boundless measure will comprise the Kingdom of Heaven. Right now, when we look around we see anything but the Kingdom of Heaven. Does it mean that the Christ has given up his promise to mankind? No, not in the least. His promise is now flowing like a river in and through each individual seeker on earth. The Kingdom of Heaven must come into existence—either today or tomorrow, either in the near future or in the distant future. The promise of the Savior Christ will definitely be fulfilled in the course of human evolution.

No God-promise can remain unfulfilled. The promise that God made to mankind through Sri Krishna, the promise that God made to mankind through the Buddha, the promise that God made to mankind through the Christ, the promises that God is offering to mankind through you, through me, through each individual seeker, will all be fulfilled.

A New Teacher: The Heart

We are all seekers. We are consciously seeking God's Light. There was a time when we did not seek God's Light, even unconsciously. Now we are consciously seeking, but previously we did not seek at all.

We are all students. Previously we were students also, but at that time our teacher was the *mind*. Now we have a new teacher, and that teacher is the *heart*. Our previous teacher asked us to walk along the desire-road. As we were students, we walked along the desire-road in order to attain the satisfaction which the teacher promised us, for it is satisfaction that makes life meaningful and fruitful. But to our surprise, the mind could not offer us satisfaction. Each time we took a step ahead, instead of satisfaction, our destination was all frustration; instead of real happiness, it was false, totally false pleasure. We previously tried to please the mind so that we could derive happiness from life, but there was no happiness on that road. We were totally dissatisfied and therefore, we changed teachers.

Now we have a new teacher, the heart. The new teacher tells us that we can and shall get happiness only if we please God in God's own Way. The new teacher tells us that we can never achieve happiness unless we become one with happiness itself, and this happiness is the soul in us.

The mind does not have happiness. If I do not have something, how can I give you that very thing? Because the mind has no happiness, it cannot teach us. The heart says, "I cannot give you happiness, but I know someone who has happiness and who is all happiness, and this person is eager to grant you happiness. I shall take you to this happiness-reality so that you can achieve and receive as much as you want."

The heart then takes us to the soul, which is all light and delight. The heart says it does not have joy of its own; only when it becomes inseparably one with the soul, does it become really happy.

The heart says, "O seeker, you do not have an iota of happiness, and I have only limited happiness, limited joy. But I know where there is boundless happiness, and I am more than eager to take you there. As your teacher, I am telling you, O seeker, to walk along with me. I am leading you to the Source. I am guiding you, but it is up to you whether you want to find this Source. Stay in the source and you will get unlimited joy, happiness and satisfaction.

"The mind, your previous teacher, wanted to guide you in its own way. But the mind is not even aware of the destination, so how can you expect the mind to give you the message of the destination, let alone take you there? I am not the destination, but I have seen the destination, and I will take you there. Like you, O seeker, I will try to develop the capacity to receive from the Source infinite joy and happiness. Our destination is eager to give us constant satisfaction, joy and delight."

The Song Universal

The song universal is freedom. Freedom from what? Freedom from limitation, freedom from imperfection and freedom from ignorance. Man is in stark bondage. Nevertheless, man has the power deep within to cut asunder the teeming ties that have bound him and forced him to launch into the sea of uncertainty.

Four thousand years ago the Vedic seers voiced forth:

Give us freedom for our bodies.
Give us freedom for our dwelling.
Give us freedom for our life.

This soulful prayer of the Vedic seers of yore will echo and re-echo throughout Eternity in humanity's aspiring heart.

Freedom does not mean being away from home. Freedom means accepting and feeling the entire world as one's real home, as one's very own. With a view to achieving and growing into this peerless freedom, man does many things. He simply throws himself into a tornado of blind activities. But man has to learn that he has only one thing to do, and that is to discover and uncover. He has to discover the divinity within and uncover the veil of ignorance without. Likewise, man has only one thing to be: God. He has to be God the Infinite, God the Eternal and God the Immortal.

It is said that the quickest way to do many things is to do only one thing at a time. Let us start by thinking of God, concentrating on God and meditating on God, and end, if there is any end, with God-realization. This is not only the quickest way, but by far the best way.

God is Freedom. In an unparalleled way, the Isha Upanishad speaks of God the Absolute:

It moves. It moves not.
Far It is. And It is near.
Within all this It is.
It is without all this.

Man's deepest faith in God and man's boundless freedom in himself go together. Sublimely significant is the Truth that James M. Barrie offers us: "The reason why birds can fly and we can't is simply that they have perfect faith, for to have faith is to have wings."

"We walk by faith, not by sight." An aspirant, a true seeker of the infinite Freedom, has to breathe in this life-giving and life-transforming Truth that the New Testament endows us with.

Man is sick. His sickness is his ignorance. He has been suffering from this unfathomable ignorance for millennia. There is considerable Truth in what George Bernard Shaw says: "We have not lost faith, but we have transferred it from God to the medical profession."

It is high time for us to come out of our ignorance-sleep. Let us not play the fool. Let us be wise once again. Let us take back our faith in God, Who alone can and will cure our entire life and our earthly existence of this fatal ignorance-sickness.

The word "united" is hallowed. It can better be felt than described—rather, it can only be felt and cannot be described at all. "United we stand, divided we fall." We are fully aware of this maxim. What we need is to live it.

Where does this unity come from? It comes from God. It comes from the *Brahman*, the One without a second. When we walk farther along the path of unity, we realize that not only does God *have* the Consciousness of Unity, but He *is* Consciousness-Unity itself. When we reach the end of our journey's Goal, we discover that God is both unity and multiplicity. In unity, God is realization and liberation; and in the field of multiplicity, He is manifestation and transformation.

Our inner realization and outer action must run abreast. Our outer achievements should be the conscious and spontaneous revelation of our inner divinity.

Love, harmony, peace and oneness: these are man's divine ideals. On the strength of his inner mounting flame of aspiration, man can easily, unerringly and spontaneously manifest these ideals of his in every sphere of his life.

It is quite natural and proper that we should discover our God in and through our own religion. When we go deep within, we come to realize that there is only one religion, and that religion is man's inmost cry for God-realization. In the hoary past, Asoka, the great Emperor of India, sent missionaries to the corners of the globe with a profound message: "The basis of all religions is the same, wherever they are. Try to help them all you can, teach them all you can, and do not try to injure them."

Let each religion play the role of a flower. Let us make a garland of these divine flowers and offer them at the Feet of God. God will be pleased. We shall be fulfilled.

As there is only one religion, even so there is only one song. This song is man.

> Man is Infinity's Heart.
> Man is Eternity's Breath.
> Man is Immortality's Life.

4

Cultivating the Fruits of the Soul

"I welcome your initiative to give a symbolic expression to our common efforts for a world in which nations will live in peace and harmony."

Vaclav Havel
President of the Czech Republic
Shown in a meeting on November 25, 1993

Chancellor Kohl holds aloft the Sri Chinmoy Peace Torch on June 4, 1995 while traveling in Egypt. The German leader offered the Peace Run participants his most heartfelt encouragement.

Helmut Kohl
Chancellor of Germany
June 4, 1995

Freedom

Freedom is the creative force within us. Freedom is the sustaining life within us. Human freedom is an experience of the body, in the vital and for the mind. Divine freedom is an experience of the soul, in the heart and for the mind, the vital and the body.

God's Freedom lies in His constant service and unconditional self-giving to mankind. Man's freedom lies in his God-achievement, life-perfection and life-fulfillment.

The freedom of the doubting mind is undoubtedly a reality. But this reality is fleeting, flimsy. The freedom of the loving and aspiring heart is an everlasting reality and an ultimate sublimity.

Freedom of earthly thought is good, but quite often it opens itself to false freedom. Freedom that comes from following the Heavenly Will invokes God's Presence in us. It invokes His divine Promise in and through us and His supreme Self-manifestation in and through us.

What is false freedom? False freedom is our constant and deliberate acceptance of ignorance and our conscious existence in ignorance. What is real freedom? Real freedom is our conscious awareness of our inner divinity and our constant inseparable oneness with the Inner Pilot.

What can false freedom do? False freedom can do much. It can totally destroy us. It can destroy our inner possibilities and potentialities. It can destroy our inner wealth. What can real freedom do? Real freedom also can do much. Real freedom can make us grow into the very image of our Supreme Pilot.

Outer freedom and inner freedom. Outer freedom constantly wants to prove its capacity and its sovereignty. Inner freedom wants to prove that it belongs to God and God alone.

Outer freedom has a new goal every day. It wants to discover this goal only in pleasure. Inner freedom has only one

eternal Goal, and that Goal is to achieve the conscious awareness of God and the conscious manifestation of God in and
through itself.

Outer freedom is satisfied only when it is in a position to
say, "I have no superiors. I am my only master." Inner freedom is satisfied only when it can soulfully say, "I don't want
to be superior to anyone. I want God to be my only Master."

Forgetfulness takes away our freedom, but God's
Forgiveness brings it back. Teeming desires take away our
freedom, but God's Compassion brings it back. Self-
importance and self-assertion take away our freedom, but
God's Light brings it back.

It is our self-awareness that retains our freedom and God's
divine Pride in us that perfects our freedom. In the perfection
of our earthly freedom we grow, and we sow the Heaven-seed
within us. In the fulfillment of our inner freedom we see
Heaven and earth as complementary souls. Earth offers its
wealth and capacity, which is receptivity, and Heaven offers
its wealth and capacity, which are divinity and Immortality.

Joy

Joy within is always a rarity.
Joy without is almost an impossibility.
Joy in oneness with God is a constant certainty
and an eternal reality.

Joy within is always a rarity. Most of us are living in the world of desire. We have no time to go deep within. There are people who feel that they do not have even one minute in a day, one single minute out of 24 hours, to go deep within. Then there are those who have the time to go deep within for a minute during the day. But when they go within, they do not get joy. Our inner life is like a vast field. We have to cultivate that field like a farmer. We have to plow the inner field with our daily meditation. After we have plowed, we have to sow the seed of joy with our sincere dedication to the inner life. Then, after a few months, a year or so, we may get a real glimpse of inner joy.

We think no matter how we meditate, we will get immediate joy. But this is not true. We may get a sense of inner satisfaction, or at times a kind of vital pleasure. But real joy we get only from our deep and profound meditation. In the outer life also, when we talk and mix with people, or exchange ideas with others, we may get a kind of satisfaction or vital pleasure. But this is not real joy. Joy is something very deep, illumining and fulfilling.

When I say joy is always a rarity in the inner life, it is because we are not really crying for this inner joy. Even if we do try to go deep within for a few minutes every day, we have to know that one has to meditate with utmost sincerity for months or years in order to get real inner joy. If one tastes this inner joy even once, one is immediately transported into

Heaven for a while. When one has real inner joy, one sees that Heaven is all around him. He is in Heaven or he has become Heaven itself. This is inner joy.

In the outer world, we think that what gives us joy is the fulfillment of our desires. But if I have a desire to own a house, then when God grants my desire, immediately I become a victim to the desire to have a better house, or two houses. And when this desire, too, is fulfilled, the next moment I become a victim to still more desires. In the outer life we want only to possess—from one car to two cars, from one dollar to two dollars. The very nature of desire is to possess. We constantly try to increase our possessions. Each time a desire is fulfilled in the outer life, we discover that we are possessed by a greater and more destructive desire. In desire itself there is no end. A fulfilled desire gives us pleasure for a second, but the next moment another desire comes with tenfold power and puts us into the frying pan again. In the life of desire, satisfaction never dawns.

The difference between man and God is this: man is possessed by his little possessions, and God is released by His infinite Possessions.

When we remain in the outer world, we are taking conscious or unconscious part in the game of desire. Each moment we are opening ourselves to desire. Desire, the thief, is entering into our heart to steal away our faith in God, our love for God, our concern for God, our dedication to God, our surrender to God. When our own will becomes one with desire, everything eventually ends in destruction. But when our will becomes one with our aspiration—which is desire purified and transformed—at that time we can sit at the Feet of God. When we sit at the Feet of God and become one with God, our own will is one with God's Will. What is God's Will? God's Will is His Concern for humanity, His Love for humanity, His Cry for the perfection of humanity. When we establish our oneness with God's Will, we enter into a constant flow of joy. There we see that God the Creator, God the Creation and God the Reality are all one.

Humanity as a whole is still separated from God's Will. Every person wants something different. God has created millions and millions of people, and each one has a different idea, a different aim, a different goal. But all these ideas and goals can become one with God's Will and still have the opportunity to flourish and to fulfill themselves in multiple form. The highest joy comes from oneness with God's Will. When humanity as a whole aspires to attain this oneness with God, the multiplicity of God will be able to have the same joy as the unity of God. We do not lose our joy if we also realize our oneness with the rest of God's creation. Both the joy of multiplicity and the joy of unity we must have. When we become one with humanity and go to God together, then we get the joy of multiplicity. And when we go directly to God alone, then we get the joy of unity. Again, from the joy of unity, we can approach God's infinite multiplicity by going to God alone and then bringing God to the rest of humanity. Then again, we get boundless inner and outer joy.

Right now the outer life and the inner life are like the North and South Pole. It seems impossible that they will ever meet. The inner life has more light than the outer life, but this light is not enough to satisfy us. Right now the inner light that we have is not strong enough to illumine and transform the outer life. In spite of knowing that the inner life has more light, the outer life stubbornly does not surrender to it. The outer life does not want to abide by the dictates of the inner life; it does not even want to cooperate with the inner life. The inner life has almost unlimited light and joy, while the outer life has practically none. But a day will come when we will get joy from the outer life. When the inner life and the outer life embrace the same goal and are ready to be consciously dedicated to the Will of God, at that time we will find joy within and joy without.

The outer life and the inner life have to become one. Both have to feel the necessity of their oneness with God. If the inner life listens to the dictates of the soul and the outer life listens to the dictates of the inner life, then the inner life and the outer life will run towards God together. At that time we will have abiding joy, everlasting joy, both here on earth and there in Heaven. Our outer life will be totally transformed, and our inner life will be constantly aspiring to be one with the infinite and ever-transcending Joy of God.

The Outer Power and
the Inner Power

Each human being on earth embodies the outer power and the inner power. He is aware of his outer power when he looks without. He is conscious of his inner power when he dives deep within. When he identifies with the mind and the body-consciousness, he is the outer power. When he identifies with the soul and its light, he is the inner power.

The body-consciousness has light of its own. The soul-consciousness has light of its own. The body-consciousness, because of its limitations, does not see far. For the body-consciousness, the future always remains a far cry. The soul-consciousness, because of its unlimited capacity, at one and the same time sees, grows into and becomes the achievements of the past, the realizations of the present and the vision-dreams of the future.

The outer power blinds the human in us. The outer power is devoured by the animal in us. The inner power clears and expands our vision; it shows our vision the way to reach the highest transcendental Goal.

The outer power is competition, conscious and constant competition. The inner power is conception, conscious conception of its own worth, its own reality and divinity. Divinity proceeds and succeeds, succeeds and proceeds. Reality eternally is. In its silence-life, reality is at once the transcendental Height and the immanent-Light.

The outer power is supremacy. The inner power is accuracy. The inner power accurately knows what it has and what it is. What it has is the source and what it is, is the manifestation of the Source.

The outer power sings with imagination, dances with

temptation and dies in frustration. The inner power practices concentration, meditation and contemplation. Concentration accepts the challenges of life. Meditation purifies and illumines the challenges of life. Contemplation transforms the challenges of life into golden opportunities.

The outer power wants to strike, and then immediately wants to escape. The inner power wants not only to embrace the world, but also to convince the world that the world's existence and its own existence are eternally inseparable.

The outer power says to the inner power, "Look what I have. I have the capacity to destroy God's entire creation." The inner power says to the outer power, "Look what I have. I have the power to illumine God's entire creation."

The outer power is at times afraid of its own creation: the atom bomb and the hydrogen bomb. The inner power is constantly feeding its creation with love-light, concern-light and perfection-light.

The outer power feels that there is a height which has to be transcended, and that if this goal is achieved, satisfaction will dawn. The inner power feels that height and depth, the foot of the mountain and the top of the mountain, are all at one place. It sees that they are singing the song of one reality, that they are all inside the cosmic Heart in perfect union, enjoying inseparable oneness.

The outer power wants only to ascend. It is afraid of descending. The inner power wants to ascend and descend. It knows perfectly well that when it is descending, it is carrying down to earth the descending God, and when it is ascending, it is carrying up to Heaven the ascending man.

The outer power is the dance of sound. The inner power is the song of silence. The life of sound is the creation of the human in us. The life of silence is the creation of the divine in us.

The outer power is the human power. The inner power is the divine power. The outer power says, "I can do. I need no help, no assistance." The inner power says, "I can do nothing and I am nothing. At the same time, I can do everything and

I am everything, because there is someone in me, the Inner Pilot, who is everything and who will do everything in and through me."

When we live in the desire-world, the world of possession and frustration, the outer power lords it over us. When we live in the aspiration-world, the world of expansion and satisfaction, the inner power illumines us and fulfills us.

The desire-world is the world of outer power. The aspiration-world is the world of inner power. Realization has a free access to both the outer power and the inner power. What is realization? Realization is the acceptance of reality as it is in the outer world and reality at its ultimate height, as it is in the inner world.

Confidence

We are all God's chosen children. God has perfect faith in us. Let us try to have an iota of divine confidence in ourselves.

If we want to have confidence, we have to be true to ourselves. If we want to hear from God that we are good, great and divine, then we must always be true to ourselves.

Temptation, depression, frustration and destruction go together. Man's confidence and God's acceptance go together. Man's confidence is man's joy and God's divine Pride.

Confidence is growth. It is the flowering of our human aspiration into divine liberation. Aspiration is what man has and what he offers to God. Liberation is what God eternally is, and He offers Himself to mankind.

Confidence is the illumining consciousness deep within us of our fulfilling inheritance. God says to man, "My child, I have all confidence in you because you are of Me." Man says to God, "Father, I have full confidence in myself because You are for me."

God says to man, "My child, I have all confidence in you because you want the Truth and the Truth alone." Man says to God, "Father, I have full confidence in myself because I know that You are the Truth and You are within me and for me."

God says to man, "My child, I have all confidence in you because of our present divine conversation." Man says to God, "Father, Father, Father, I have full confidence in myself because of Your present and eternal Compassion for me."

Simplicity, Sincerity and Purity

Simplicity, sincerity and purity. On the one hand, these three qualities we are able to use at any moment in our day-to-day life. On the other hand, they are the most difficult qualities to achieve. It takes only a few seconds to spell "simplicity," "sincerity" and "purity." But these are not mere words, not mere ideas or conceptions. They represent three illumining and fulfilling worlds: the world of simplicity, the world of sincerity and the world of purity.

Each individual on earth is running towards a destination. If the runner is simple, he will wear only the basic garments that are necessary. He will not wear something very heavy or expensive to draw the attention of the spectators. If the runner is sincere, then he will run in his own lane. He will not enter into other's lanes and thus disturb them and create confusion in them. If the runner is pure, then in silence he will conquer the spectators' hearts. By being simple, sincere and pure he will run the fastest. And while he is running, there will come a time when he will feel that the goal itself has been within his easy reach right from the beginning.

Each time an individual is simple, he feels an extra amount of peace and joy inside his restless mind. Each time an individual is sincere, he feels that he has gained a considerable portion of the length and breadth of the world. Each time an individual is pure, he feels that the whole world is not only in him, but also for him.

Each human being, no matter how old he is, how mature he is, how developed he is, how intelligent he is, if he wants to have an iota of peace, abiding peace, he must have simplicity, sincerity and purity. These are the three qualities that are most essential in each individual life and also in the collective life of humanity.

There are people who are of the opinion that simplicity is almost tantamount to stupidity. But I wish to say that simplicity and stupidity are like North Pole and South Pole. One can be as simple as a child and, at the same time, one can have boundless knowledge, light and wisdom. The great philosopher Socrates is a striking example. He embodied both simplicity and wisdom. And in his case, we can see something more. He was not only a man of simplicity, but also a man of inner sincerity and inner purity.

Each human being wants satisfaction. Satisfaction in life can come only by acquiring wisdom, more wisdom, abundant wisdom, infinite wisdom. In order to achieve infinite wisdom, we have to become students. Socrates, the great philosopher, a man of boundless wisdom, said, "I would like to be an eternal student." A child's life is the life of a student. A child feels at every moment that he has something new to learn to become. A child grows; he opens his mind's door to world-knowledge and his heart's door to world-experience. And each time he learns something, he feels there is something more he has to learn.

All those who are working at the United Nations or working for the United Nations are serving the world individually and collectively according to their capacities. But if we want to increase this capacity, either in the physical world, the vital world, the mental world or the psychic world, then we all have to feel that we are students, that we are children.

The United Nations is at once the body and the soul of God's unique Vision. Those of us who serve the body and the soul of God's Vision will be blessed divinely, supremely, unreservedly and infinitely—but only when we feel the necessity of seeing in ourselves a child's heart, feeling in ourselves a child's life. The dreamer in us is a child. He dreams of God's infinite Peace, Light and Bliss. Today's dream-life will tomorrow grow into reality-experience and reality-satisfaction.

The more we feel the necessity of simplicity, sincerity and purity, the more we become perfect instruments—not only of the nations that we represent, but also of the Almighty, whom we represent here on earth. Let us become simple. Let us become sincere. Let us become pure. If we can become simple, sincere and pure, then not only will the dreams that we treasure for our own countries soon be fulfilled, but also all the dreams that the Almighty has for His own manifestation will be manifested in and through us. At that time we shall grow into His Reality-Satisfaction and Reality-Perfection.

Simplicity, sincerity, purity: right now they are our most faithful, devoted instruments to help us reach the ultimate Goal. There will come a day when we see that our Goal of the transcendental Height is smiling in and through these three faithful and devoted friends of ours. And in this transcendental Smile we will see and feel that we are not mere mortals subjected to ignorance-life, but rather we are part and parcel of Infinity's Light, Eternity's Love and Immortality's all-embracing, all-illumining and all-fulfilling Oneness.

Patience

Patience is our unrecognized capacity; patience is our unrecognized achievement. Capacity succeeds; achievement proceeds. Patience is our soul's light. This light is always unconditional.

Physical power, vital power and mental power are no match for patience-power. When physical power is misused against someone, the patience-power of that person can eventually triumph. In the outer life and the inner life, patience-power will eventually succeed. Human power is in no way different from destructive animal power if we do not aspire, if we do not long for truth, light and beauty.

God created this world. In His vast creation He considers patience to be His dear friend. God and His Patience are inseparable. God's creation is not complete; perfection is still a far cry. God, with His infinite Patience-Light, aspires for perfection in and through each creation of His. God feels that His Patience-Light has a divine, magic power that can transform the dark past into the golden future.

Man needs patience in order to discover what he truly is. God needs patience in order to make man feel not only that he is God's son, God's dearest creation, but also that he is exactly the same as God. Man has to realize what he eternally is: God Himself. Man is now God veiled; with patience-light man will unveil his inner divinity. Man is God yet to be consciously and constantly realized, and God is man yet to be manifested totally, completely and unmistakably here on earth.

Deliberately and consciously man claims something as his own which is not actually his: ignorance. There is only one thing that man can truly claim as his own: God. Nothing less and nothing more. Unless and until man comes to realize this, he will never know who he is. Man is Divinity's reality. This is the only thing that he has to discover: his real reality, which is dormant within him.

Even when he is in the desire-life, each man should realize that within him is the God-seed. That God-seed is going to germinate eventually into a plant, and from a plant it will grow into a huge banyan tree. Again, when the same person enters into the spiritual life, he has to feel that the fruit, the eternal fruit, is already there for him to eat. In the desire-world he has to discover God the seed so that he can grow and grow in aspiration. In the aspiration-world he has to discover God the fruit so that he can recognize what he eternally is.

Patience is our revealing and revealed faith in God, the Supreme Pilot, and our revealed and revealing faith in our own existence. Patience is our faith in our own discovery that we are not only of God but also for God.

The human cry that climbs up from the inmost recesses of our heart makes friends with patience in order to see the smiling face of the Eternal Pilot. Again, the Eternal Pilot makes friends with patience so that one day He will see in humanity's cry the perfect liberation, everlasting salvation, complete illumination and total transformation of humanity.

God's Brightest Heaven and
Man's Surest Haven

Of all the divine qualities, unfortunately light is wanted the least, even though it is needed most by all. People want love, peace, joy and power, but very rarely do they consciously want Light. Unconsciously or consciously, they are afraid of light. They feel that the effulgence of light will expose their imperfections, limitations and bondage. They fear that the power of divine light will forcefully uproot the ignorance-tree that they embody.

Neither of these fears is true. The divine light embraces the world in all its ignorance. Further, the divine light feels that it is its bounden duty to elevate the human consciousness until it can receive the plenitude of the life divine. If we really want to live a divine life on earth, then we have to cry, cry like a child for God's Compassion-Light, which is at once God's brightest Heaven and man's surest haven.

The Role of Humility

In our spiritual life, in our life of aspiration and dedication, humility is the root, divinity is the tree and Immortality is the fruit.

The perfect man is he whose inner being is flooded with humility. It is he who eventually becomes God's transcendental Choice and God's universal Voice.

Humility and self-conceit are two real strangers to each other. Humility and God-awareness are two eternal friends. Humility and divinity's reality-expansion are eternally inseparable, inseparably one.

When I am humble to my inferiors, they adore me. When I am humble to my equals, they love me. When I am humble to my superiors, they appreciate me. When I am humble to God, He claims me as His best instrument on earth.

To climb up God's Vision-Tree I need only one thing: humility's beauty. To climb down God's Reality-Tree I need only one thing: humility's magnanimity.

There are many roads that lead to God. There is one road which is by far the shortest and, at the same time, most illumining, and that road is the humility-road.

Self-Giving and Happiness

A seeker need not be an individual who only cries and tries to realize God. A seeker can be someone who sees something that he does not have right now. He wants something that will give him joy and satisfaction in life, but he does not have that very thing. In order to become proficient in anything, deep inside us we have to have a sincere inner cry. We want to do something, to grow into something, to become something. This means we are seekers.

Each profession is like a good quality that we can offer to the world at large, a quality that can satisfy and fulfill us. We have a human family, and in that family one member is a doctor, another member is a teacher, a third is a lawyer and a fourth can be a something else. All feel an illumining and fulfilling bond among them. Each one plays his respective role in the family and in the world. The skill and capacity of each one is needed. The self-offering of each one is of paramount importance.

Each profession is a signal capacity of God. If we are uncomfortable using the term "God," let us use the term "happiness." Each capacity offers us happiness. If someone is endowed with a special capacity, that means he can give and receive happiness through that capacity, and this happiness encourages him to go forward. In his own life he embodies capacity, he represents capacity and he manifests capacity for the satisfaction of human life, both his own and others', on earth.

Each individual has some special quality. That means he has capacity in abundant measure, in boundless measure. Yet, as individuals, we are not perfectly happy, in spite of having capacity in one particular field. How can we be happy? We can be happy only if we believe in progress. We have to change ourselves in order to grow inwardly and outwardly. We have to change what we have and what we are in order to make progress.

What do we have? We have the physical body, the vital, the mind and the heart. Right now the body is unconscious. The vital is aggressive. The mind is doubtful. The heart is insecure. The body is unconscious like a solid wall. The vital is aggressive like a hungry wolf. The mind is doubtful like a doubting Thomas. The heart is insecure like a child in the woods. But all this can be changed, transformed. We can have a conscious body, a dynamic vital, a believing mind and a secure heart if we cry inwardly for something higher and better.

What are we? We are followers of the neutral life. We feel that we are not in a position to know right from wrong, that we are not in a position to judge, or we feel that the only way to achieve peace is to surrender or compromise. But this is a deplorable mistake. Compromise can never give us abiding joy. He who compromises is consciously surrendering his ideals. Someone who is neutral is not sure of what the truth is or what the truth looks like. We know we are in between ignorance-night and wisdom-light. It is up to us to discover and accept wisdom, and to free ourselves totally from the snares of ignorance.

Everything that we feel will make us happy in life eventually disappoints us or deserts us, with the exception of one thing, and that thing is Truth. To live in Truth is to live in happiness. There are various ways to achieve Truth in our life, but only one way is most effective. That way is the way of self-giving—unreserved and unconditional self-giving to our own extended, expanded, enlarged, boundless, unlimited existence.

When we enter into our unlimited existence, we feel that we are of the One and for the many. At the same time, we feel that we are of the many and for the One. This moment we are the tree; the next moment we are the leaves. The tree needs branches, leaves, flowers and fruits in order to prove to the world that it is actually a tree. And the leaves need the trunk and branches to prove to the world that they are part and parcel of the tree.

Each profession is a branch of the life-tree. At the same time each profession has to feel that there is a root to the capacity-tree. If there is no root, then there can be no branches, leaves, fruits and so forth. The root of the life-tree is happiness. How can we live with happiness as our source all the time? Only by self-giving: by generously giving what we have and what we are. What we have is capacity and what we are is oneness. By offering our capacity in any form to mankind—to our so-called superiors and so-called inferiors, or to our brothers and sisters of the world—we come to know what we ultimately and eternally are: oneness inseparable.

I Shall Not Avoid

I shall not avoid you anymore, O my weak body. Now I know how I can transform you. I shall ask my dynamic vital to come and play with you for some time every day. In this way, without fail, you will become strong.

I shall not avoid you anymore, O my impure vital. Now I know how I can transform you. I shall ask my intelligent mind to come and spend some time with you every day. I am sure you will take the intelligent and wise advice that my mind will give you. In this way, without fail, your impurity will be transformed into purity.

I shall not avoid you anymore, O my doubting mind. Now I know how I can transform you. I shall ask my soulful heart, my childlike heart, to come and play with you for at least two hours every day. My soulful, childlike heart will undoubtedly be able to change you, O my doubting mind, and transform your doubts into sterling faith. In this way, without fail, you will become a soulful and faithful mind.

I shall not avoid you anymore, O my insecure heart. Now I know how I can transform you. I shall ask my all-knowing soul to grant you its security-ocean. I am sure it will abide by my request. In this way, without fail, all your insecurity will be transformed into security-confidence-ocean.

I shall not avoid you anymore, O my unfulfilled soul. Now I know how I can help you. I have the answer, the answer of answers. I shall pray to my Beloved Supreme to grant you more wisdom-light and more perfection-delight so that you can unmistakably fulfill yourself here on earth. In this way, without fail, you will be able to fulfill your promise to the Supreme.

I shall not avoid You anymore, O my Beloved Supreme.

Now I shall be able to satisfy You. My entire being is now enjoying the beauty, the purity and divinity of a new awakening, a new dawn. I have grown into a new awakening, and this new awakening has given me a new light. From now on my body, vital, mind, heart and soul—both individually and collectively—will have only one name: gratitude. I know that herein lies the answer. In this way, my Beloved Supreme, without fail, I shall be able to please You in Your own Way and I shall be able to address You by another name. Satisfaction Supreme. O my Beloved Supreme, when gratitude becomes the name of my body, vital, mind, heart and soul, at that time You will have another name: Satisfaction Supreme.

5

God
Within
and
Without

On being awarded the Gandhi Peace Award, along with Sri Chinmoy: *"I accept this award, humbled that you have chosen me along with such an esteemed spiritual leader as Sri Chinmoy."*

Coretta Scott King
President, Martin Luther King, Jr. Center
for Nonviolent Social Change
October 28, 1994

From a letter to Sri Chinmoy on the dedication of Ottawa as a Sri Chinmoy Peace Capital: *"Congratulations on the dedication of the city of Ottawa as a peace capital. I am confident that this gesture will help in making the people and their leaders more aware about the importance of peace."*

The Dalai Lama
Spiritual leader of the Tibetan Buddhists
and Nobel Peace Laureate
Shown prayerfully blessing the Peace Torch in Scotland
May 15, 1993

God's Power of Love in Today's World

God's Power of Love has three gifts to offer: aspiration, liberation and perfection. Man's power of love also has three gifts to offer: possession, frustration and destruction.

God's Power of Love in today's world can be felt only by the special few who have discovered the inner truth that love is the beauty of our aspiring life and the duty of our manifesting soul.

The body of today's world is like a filthy pig. The vital of today's world is like a mad elephant. The mind of today's world is like a devouring tiger. The heart of today's world is like a timid deer. The soul of today's world is like a helpless lamb.

In supreme silence, God's Power of Love is performing its eternal divine Duty. Slowly, steadily and unerringly, it is transforming the body, the filthy pig, into a clean and pure child; the vital, the mad elephant, into a one-pointed dynamic runner; the mind, the devouring tiger, into a seeker of the highest Truth; the heart, the timid deer, into a brother of boundless confidence and concern; and the soul, the helpless lamb, into a chosen instrument of Divinity's Eternity.

The master philosopher Plato described love as "a great mental disease." When our physical consciousness lives in the doubting, suspecting and unaspiring mind, this description is, to some extent, undeniable. But if our awakened consciousness lives in the illumining soul, love is nectar, the very breath of Immortality.

Napoleon Bonaparte offered us an amusing and interesting piece of advice: "The only victory over love is flight." When our human emotions run riot, the necessity of flying away is perhaps indispensable. But when divine emotion, the pure, all-loving emotion, reigns supreme, we do not need victory *over* love, but the victory *of* love. This victory of love is self-expansion in God-manifestation.

India's matchless leader Mahatma Gandhi called love "the reverse of the coin of which the obverse is Truth." In the life of aspiration we come to realize that love is Truth embodied, and that Truth is love revealed.

Man's pervasive ignorance of divine love results in a most damaging failure in the battlefield of life. Man's power of love is constantly wanting in purity and lucidity. Man's love of power knows not how to be patient. Fast, faster and fastest it runs; and when it finally reaches its goal, it is compelled to shake hands with bitter frustration. Earthly experience, frustrated and shattered, convinces a lover that there is no such thing as love. But Heavenly experience, illumining and fulfilling, reveals to a God-lover the truth that divine love alone is worthwhile here on earth, there in Heaven.

An unaspiring man loves God in a perfunctory manner. An aspiring man loves God in a soulful and unreserved manner. A God-realized man loves God in an unconditionally surrendered manner. It is through him that God, the Inner Pilot Supreme, reveals His Power of Love in today's world.

No Chance but God's Concern

No chance but God's Concern. No golden chance but God's constant Concern. There is no such thing as chance. There is only God's constant, selfless, unreserved Concern. This Concern is His glowing, flowing and descending Grace.

Before I act, I need to live. Before I live, I need to breathe. Before I breathe, I need to know the purpose of my life, the aim of my earthly existence. If the ultimate aim of my earthly existence is to reach the farthest, feel the deepest and climb the highest, then I have to breathe God's Light in and out from God Himself.

From whom can I have God's Light? God's Light I can have directly from God when the fleeting moment of my unconditionally surrendered life I offer to God.

When can I have God's Light? I can have God's Light when I am consciously aware of the undeniable fact that God loves me infinitely more than I love Him, and also that God loves me infinitely more than I love myself.

How can I have God's Light? I can have God's Light when I grow into the purest humility of the poor and the mightiest magnanimity of the rich. My humility is my divine brotherhood. My magnanimity is my divine fatherhood.

I have to feel that it is God, God alone, who constantly cares for me. I am not afraid of speaking the truth to the world because I feel that God is speaking through me. I am not afraid of working in the world because I feel that God is acting through me. I am not afraid of transforming the world-nature because I know that God is doing it for me. Finally, I am not afraid of affirming that God and I are eternally and perpetually one because God has confided in me that there can be no higher Truth than this.

God is Concern. This Concern enters into the darkening ignorance of humanity to transform the face of the world only when the earth-consciousness is ready to receive God's spontaneous, constant and unreserved Concern soulfully and unreservedly.

No chance but God's Concern. No golden chance but God's constant Concern.

God and Truth

God expresses Himself through Silence. God expands Himself through Light. God unites Himself with His Creation through Delight.

Man's outer life needs God's Silence. Man's inner life needs God's Light. Man's higher life needs God's Delight.

Yet, man is God's Hope. Man is God's Smile. Man is God's Pride. Man is God's Hope in his inner life, man is God's Smile in his higher life and man is God's Pride in his outer life.

God's Hope is man's possibility. God's Smile is man's ability. God's Pride is man's necessity.

Truth, the ultimate Truth, plays its role in three different stages of evolution: objective, subjective and absolute. In the objective stage, Truth is man's searching consciousness. In consciousness man sees the Truth in its practical form. In the subjective stage, Truth is man's awakening Divinity. In Divinity man sees the truth in its theoretical form. And in the absolute stage, Truth is man's fulfilling Reality. In Reality man sees the Truth in its universal form.

The Court of Divine Justice

The court of human justice tells me that as I sow, so I reap. The court of divine justice assures me that when I devotedly think of God, He smilingly and blessingfully appears before my heart's eye.

Human justice wishes to offer me protection. Human justice is fairness. Human justice is a threatening force. Human justice is a binding law. Divine justice offers me protection, illumination and perfection. Divine justice is Love. Divine justice is self-giving. Divine justice is fulfillment.

The human judge is the problem-shooter. The human plaintiff is the problem-bringer. The human defendant is the problem-maker. The human advocate is either the problem-lover or problem-nourisher; he cannot be otherwise, for that is how he remains on earth.

The divine judge is the liberator. In the divine sense the plaintiff is the hungry seeker, the defendant is the devouring doubter and the advocate is conscience. This advocate is the common friend of both the plaintiff and the defendant. Under threat from wild ignorance, the advocate sometimes yields to the forces of human weakness; but inwardly it loves, cherishes and serves only Truth. In the physical and vital worlds, conscience may be helpless, but in the inner world, conscience is constantly supported by the adamantine Will of the Lord Supreme.

Justice is impartiality. Impartiality is wisdom. Wisdom is divine Grace. Divine Grace is the illumining Vision and fulfilling manifestation of God.

God's Consciousness abides in the duty of His divine Justice. A transformed and perfected human being is the duty of divine justice. A fulfilled and manifested God in man is the duty of divine justice. Duty performed on any level of con-sciousness is beauty blossomed forthwith.

On the human level, liberty and justice are two different things. One can enjoy complete liberty while at the same time violating all the laws of justice. One can enjoy liberty, espe-cially on the vital plane, with no regard for justice at all. But again, if one cares only for justice, then we feel there is no pleasure, no warmth, no feeling of enthusiasm in his life. This is all on the human level.

In the inner world, on the divine level, liberty and justice always go together. They are like the obverse and reverse of the same coin. Only he who has inner freedom can fully understand the message of divine justice. Only he who knows what divine justice is can be truly free and independent. Liberty and justice in the inner world are inseparable.

Divine justice is not a mere human idea. It is a divine ideal in each human being. When a nation is not awakened, when a nation is unaspiring and unillumined, it feels that might is right. This is human justice. But when a nation is illumined, all-loving and all-embracing, it knows that right is might. It feels that justice lies only in right action. What is right action? Right action is the conscious feeling of universal oneness.

God's Justice can be truly known and acted upon only when we have the feeling of universal oneness. Our human mind will never be able to fathom God's Justice. It will always be baffled by God's Justice because of its limited knowledge and limited concern for humanity.

Divine justice is ready at every moment to help us, inspire us, guide us, mold us and shape us. But we are equally afraid of divine justice and human justice. When we do something wrong, we feel that we will be exposed and punished. This is true in the case of human justice, but divine justice does not expose us. The first time we do something wrong, divine jus-tice will forgive us with its compassion. The second time we do something wrong, it will offer us more compassion. The third time we do something wrong, it will offer us infinite compassion. Finally, when God sees that even His infinite

Compassion does not solve the human problem, He will use His loving divine Authority, His divine Power.

Divine power is not destructive power. This power is not threatening power. This power is the power that awakens the dormant lion in each human being. This power does not want to dominate or punish. It wants only to arouse the spiritually hungry lion in each human being. This lion can roar, but right now it is fast asleep. This lion is our inner cry to know the ultimate Truth, to grow into the Absolute Reality.

What we have, we can give to mankind if we want to. But in God's case, He gives us not only what He has, but also what He is. He feels that He is just, only when He can give us what He has and what He is. We can also act like God and offer to mankind not only what we have, but also what we are. When we make an inner search, we come to learn that what we have is a dedicated heart, and that we are the chosen instruments of God.

Divine justice is the breath of Reality. In the human court we see all kinds of crime; but in the court of divine justice we notice only one crime every day, and that is human ingratitude. For that crime the punishment is forgiveness. Constantly a game is being played between God's Forgiveness and man's ingratitude. In a human way, human beings justify their cause by saying, "We are unconscious, hence we commit crimes. We are not yet illumined, hence we are ungrateful." In a divine way, God justifies His cause: He is Love, hence He is all-loving. He is Forgiveness, hence He is all-forgiving.

God: The Supreme Actor;
World: The Divine Audience

God: the Supreme Actor. World: the divine audience. The Supreme Actor reveals His Love. The Supreme Actor fulfills His Truth. The divine audience believes. The divine audience achieves. Self-awakening is the belief of the divine audience. God-discovery is the achievement of the divine audience.

The Supreme Actor acts three times a day. In the morning, the Supreme Actor offers inspiration-light to us. In the afternoon, the Supreme Actor offers aspiration-height to us. In the evening, the Supreme Actor offers realization-might to us.

In the inspiration-light of the Supreme Actor, the divine audience sees that the attainment of the ultimate Truth is quite possible. In the aspiration-height of the Supreme Actor, the divine audience feels that the attainment of the ultimate Truth is not only possible, but also practical. In the realization-might of the Supreme Actor, the divine audience realizes that the attainment of the ultimate Truth is not only possible and practical, but also natural and inevitable.

The divine audience looks at the Feet of the Supreme Actor and longs for the liberation of mankind from ignorance. The divine audience looks at the Eyes of the Supreme Actor and longs for the perfect Perfection of aspiring humanity.

The Supreme Actor enters into the head of the divine audience to encourage its lofty ideals. The Supreme Actor enters into the heart of the divine audience to glorify its divinity's light and reality's delight.

Believable: the human audience is afraid of devouring darkness. Unbelievable, but true: the human audience is afraid of illumining light.

The divine audience is always proud of seeing the light of

God's Beauty. The divine audience is always proud of feeling the Delight of God's Beauty,

The soul is an actor. The soul participates in the cosmic *Lila*, the divine Game, by entering into the abyss of ignorance. The soul enters into the chasm of inconscience in order to participate in the cosmic *Lila*. For millennia the soul abides there, fast asleep. Then all of a sudden a spark of consciousness enters into the soul and awakens it. The soul makes a little movement. At that very moment a question arises from within: "Who am I?" The immediate answer also comes from within: *Tat twam asi*, "That thou art."

The soul opens its eyes, looks upward and enters into the mineral world. There again, for thousands and thousands of years the soul abides. Then the soul again gets a question from within: "Who am I?" The answer is again, *Tat twam asi*, "That thou art." The soul makes another upward movement. From the mineral world, the soul enters into the plant world for millennia. From there it enters into the animal kingdom, where again for hundreds of years the soul is not fully active or dynamic. Very often it is fast asleep, enjoying the cosmic Game in its own particular fashion.

But there comes a time, after hundreds of years, when the soul wants to go one step farther in the evolving wheel of manifestation. The soul enters into human life. Here the soul becomes either unconsciously active or consciously dynamic. Here the soul gets more opportunity, develops more capacity to look up high into the Beyond. Here the soul has the opportunity to remember its Source, the ultimate Truth, the transcendental Reality.

The soul entered into inconscience to begin the Game. The soul, from the human incarnation, enters into the full consciousness of divine life so that it can eventually go back to its Source: *Sat-Chit-Ananda*, Existence-Consciousness-Bliss.

Each soul is employed by humanity and Divinity. In God's cosmic Drama, humanity employs the soul to carry its untold suffering and excruciating pangs to a world far beyond the domain of the mind. Divinity employs the soul to bring the message of light and delight down into the very heart of the earth-consciousness. Divinity asks the soul to be the boatman so that Divinity can manifest its Infinity in the heart of the finite. Humanity asks the soul to be its boat so that it can carry the burden of humanity to the world beyond.

The Supreme Actor is the Beloved Sovereign. The divine audience is the eternal lover. Both the Actor and the audience are indispensable, one fulfilling the other. The audience is receiving and achieving the ultimate Truth. The Actor is receiving and manifesting the ultimate Truth.

The Supreme Actor is also the Supreme Dancer. When Lord Shiva Nataraj, the Supreme Dancer, dances, lo and behold, humanity's aspiration is being awakened, humanity's unlit consciousness is being illumined, Divinity's life-breath is being manifested on earth. When Lord Krishna, the Supreme Dancer, dances, lo and behold, humanity's passion is being transformed into Divinity's rapture.

The Supreme Actor wants each individual soul to become the Supreme Actor in the play of cosmic evolution. For it is only when He allows each individual soul to play the role of the Supreme Actor that unity in multiplicity can be offered to mankind. The unity of the Supreme can be realized and manifested only when each individual soul is given the chance in the cosmic evolution to rise up high, higher, highest into the ever-transcending Beyond. Only then will God the Supreme Actor be totally fulfilled and supremely manifested here on earth.

The human actor tells the human audience, "Take me; you need me."

The human audience tells the human actor, "We do not need you. We appreciate your capacity, but we do not need your life's unreality."

The Supreme Actor tells the divine audience, "Take Me; I am for you. Take Me; I am eternally yours."

The divine audience tells the Supreme Actor, "Our devoted oneness, our surrendered oneness with You, O Supreme Actor, has made us feel the significance of Your transcendental

Reality. O Supreme Actor, to You we bow and bow. Our life of aspiration is eternally Yours. Your Life of manifestation is eternally ours."

Where Is God?

"Where is God?"

"There is no God."

If one says that there is no God, he is asserting his conception of God in a negative way. A real seeker takes the view of an atheist as sincerely and seriously as he does his own positive conception of God. A real seeker knows and feels that an atheist's conception of nothingness and the non-existence of God contains the seeker's own conception of God.

"Where is God?"

"There is no God. Even if God exists, who needs Him? Who wants Him? I can get along without God. I can remain satisfied with what I have."

When one is satisfied with what little he has, that means that God the Happiness is making him satisfied, even with his little achievement. One can never be happy if one does not consciously or unconsciously meet with God the Happiness in each thing he sees, does and grows into.

"Where is God?"

"I am not even sure that He exists."

If one says that he is doubtful about God's existence, that means he has at least some faith in God's existence. Each human being has a friend and an enemy. His enemy, doubt, negates the living inner Truth in him. His friend, faith, feeds and strengthens his inner conception of Truth. Finally, it immortalizes the Truth in his heart, mind, vital and body.

"Where is God?"

"I do not know where God is, but I would like to know."

If someone is just curious to know about God but has no real need for God, then from the strict spiritual point of view he is not a real seeker. But if one enlarges his spiritual heart, then he embraces even that curious person and includes him in his spiritual life. He feels that today's man of curiosity can become tomorrow's man of genuine spirituality, provided he is given sincere concern, compassion, encouragement and love.

"Where is God?"

"God is all around me and within me. Now I must learn how to see Him and feel Him."

If the seeker has genuine aspiration rather than mere curiosity, he is undoubtedly on the correct path, for this is the only way to reach God. This seeker is like a child who knows that his father exists, although he may not be visible at this moment. Just as a human child feels confidence in his father's existence even when the child is at home and his father is at the office, so a spiritual seeker feels that no matter where he is, his Father is also there, somewhere in the same universal house.

At the end of knowing and feeling, we come to seeing and becoming. The spiritual seeker knows what God is and feels what God is. Then he goes deep within, sees God face to face and eventually becomes God Himself. At this point he answers the question, "Where is God?" with the question, "Where is He not?" He also answers another question, "Who is God?" with the question, "Who is not God?"

God and Goal

God and the transcendental Goal are one. In spite of their oneness, each has a distinctive role to play. The Goal is the house, and God is the Owner of the house. Since I wish to enter the house, I need permission from the Owner or I need to become the Owner. When I pray and meditate, God, out of His infinite Bounty, allows me to enter His house. If I am all appreciation and admiration for the house, if I am all adoration for the Owner, then the Owner will allow me to come inside.

If we appreciate God's creation, the house, then God feels that He Himself is being appreciated, for He and His creation are eternally one. The creation that God has revealed is His own manifestation of His Silence. If we appreciate His creation-manifestation, if we appreciate what the Creator has already revealed, then the Creator will show us that this creation of His is not and cannot be His ultimate achievement. He will elevate our consciousness and show us His unmanifested Capacity, His infinite Capacity, His Eternity and His Immortality. And He will not only show us His Infinity's Treasure, but also share it with us.

When we appreciate the creation, it is not as easy for us to reach the Highest as it is when we appreciate the Creator. If we sincerely appreciate the Creator, He gives us not only what He has already revealed, but also what He inwardly has kept aside or what He inwardly is. So although Creator and creation are inseparable, if we are wise, we shall appreciate the Creator more than the creation, for He is the Supreme Artist who reveals through His creation the Reality of His unlimited Infinity.

God is evolving. God is transcending. When He evolves, we

call Him man. Man is God in the process of His cosmic evolution. When He transcends, we call Him God. Matter is aspiring and evolving. Spirit is dancing and smiling. The smile of Spirit is what we call transcendence. When Spirit smiles, immediately we see that the earth-bound consciousness is freed from its limitations and becomes the Heaven-free Reality.

The Goal is satisfaction and perfection. Satisfaction is what we have in our achievement. But perfection is not found in our achievement; perfection is in our progressing and becoming. Progressing and becoming are founded upon our self-giving, which is the constant, conscious and all-fulfilling Reality in us and for God.

We are all seekers and we shall always remain seekers, even after we have realized God. Before we realize God, we seek God-realization; after we realize God, we seek God-manifestation. There are three principal stages in our seeking. At first we are all beginner-seekers. We feel that God is inside our hearts, but we feel that the Goal is high above us, hiding in the sky somewhere. When we pray and meditate, we feel that God is listening. Where is He? Inside our heart. Inside the heart is the soul. The soul is a spark of God's Consciousness. God is inside the building, but there is a particular room where we can see Him and always feel His Presence, and that is inside the soul.

We do not remain always beginners in our spiritual life. If we study for a few years, we do not remain in kindergarten, but go on to primary school, high school and university. In the spiritual life also, we someday become advanced seekers. When we become advanced seekers, we feel that God is inside our heart and that the Goal is also inside our heart. We feel that God and the Goal are inside our inner being and are inseparable. If we reach the house, our destination, definitely we will find the Owner there. And if we reach the Owner and He sees that we have tremendous love and devotion for Him, then He will certainly be gracious enough to take us into His house.

Eventually we reach the third stage: we become realized. When we become realized, it means that we have seen God and have been in His house. Now it is up to us, after seeing the house and the Owner, to become something. After seeing God, we become true God-lovers. At every moment we try to love God and please Him in His own Way. And after seeing the Goal, we feel that it is our bounden duty to share the Goal with others. At that time we become God-distributors. We have tasted the fruit and now we feel inspired to share the fruit with others, for only in this way can we become totally satisfied.

Earth-Experience and God-Experience

The experience of earth-life is only a moment in the flow of eternal Life. But this earth-life is not the product of earth-bound time. It is the creation of infinite Time, eternal Time. If the seeker is aware of infinite and eternal Time, then he realizes that these are nothing other than the eternal Now. God's Body, creation, is growing in the eternal Now. God's Spirit is glowing in the eternal Now.

A sincere seeker longs for God-realization. For him, God-realization means the transcendental Height, which he thinks is the height of silence, light and delight. But one may reach the highest pinnacle of Truth, without necessarily being near the highest Height. In order to achieve the highest, loftiest Height, one has to enter into the oneness-life. If one neglects or rejects God's universal Oneness-Life, then no matter how many times he reaches the highest pinnacle, he cannot be closest or nearest to God, the Highest Absolute. The height has to be scaled, but we have to know that while climbing up the mountain, we are carrying within us the universal Life, the life of multiplicity, which we are carrying to the Source, the transcendental Reality.

We speak about God and think about God, but why is it that we do not feel God as our supreme necessity, as the fulfillment of our reality? The main reason is that the earth-thoughts we treasure are composed of conscious or unconscious temptations. When temptation is fulfilled, we see nothing but futility; we see a barren desert. Since our earth-thoughts right now are nothing but futility, we cannot approach God. But there are also Heaven-thoughts. Heaven-thoughts right now are nothing short of curiosity. We are curious to know what is happening in Heaven, what it looks like, how many angels are there, what the cosmic gods are doing.

When we live on earth and think of Heaven with a curious mind, we do not realize God and accomplish our supreme task. But when we love or treasure God-thoughts at every moment in all our activities, God becomes a living Reality in our life. At every moment God's Divinity and God's Reality loom large when we feel the God-necessity in ourselves. At that time God cannot hide from us. As a matter of fact, He does not deliberately hide at all. He is nearer to us than our own eyes, but we are wanting in the cosmic vision to see Him. How can we be endowed with the cosmic vision? We can be endowed with the cosmic vision only when we feel an immediate and constant necessity for God. If we can come to feel that without food, without water, even without air we can exist, but not without God, then God-realization will not remain a far cry.

We have to know that God-realization cannot be achieved by hook or by crook, by torturing the body or the physical consciousness. If we torture our body or fast most rigorously, if we threaten God, saying, "God, if You don't come to me soon, I shall fast until death; I shall destroy my life," God will simply laugh at our stupidity. There are seekers who have fixed a date by which they have to realize God and who say they will put an end to their life if they fail. But God-realization cannot be achieved in that way.

The right method is prayer and meditation. When we pray and meditate, God observes whether our prayer and meditation are sincere or not. When He sees that we are sincere, slowly and steadily He appears before our vision. Right now He is within us, but our vision does not see Him. When we pray and meditate sincerely, He improves our vision so we can see Him and feel Him as our very own.

Besides prayer and meditation, there is another important method. We have to cry inwardly. It is through our intense inner cry that we can immediately see God face to face and have Him as our own. When we pray sincerely, when we meditate sincerely. we realize God slowly and steadily. But if inside our prayer and meditation there is also an intense inner cry, then God stands before us immediately—and not only immediately, but also unreservedly. When He sees that our inner cry is flooded with sincerity, then He becomes unconditional. First He stands in front of us, as a momentary blessing and boon, and then He becomes ours unreservedly, continuously and unconditionally.

My Captain Commands,
"Go On!"

Our life's captain is the Lord Supreme. He has given us the opportunity to live on earth with the full expectation that we will go forward, that we will make progress. But right now we have become inseparably one with the limitations of the body, the vital, the mind and the heart.

The human body tells the seeker in us, "Let us tell God that we wish to sleep for some time, and then we shall accept His Command." So the human body and the seeker tell God that they would like to enjoy sleep for a short while and then they will listen to God's Dictates.

God immediately says to the human body and the seeker in us that they can do so if they want to, but after some time He does expect them to wake up, accept Him and walk along the road of inner and outer progress. So the body and the seeker start to sleep and sleep and sleep. They do not want to wake up. Sometimes they forget to get up; sometimes they deliberately do not get up. Therefore, they do not proceed along the road of light and delight to the Golden Shore of the Beyond.

The vital and the seeker within us say to God, "Lord, we shall listen to Your Command. But before that, please allow us to fight, struggle and win. Before we proceed, before we march on towards the ultimate Goal, let us dominate and lord it over the world for a few days, a few months, a few years. After that, we shall definitely abide by Your Command; we shall walk, march and run towards the destined Goal."

God says to the vital and the seeker, "Granted. But don't forget that after you have fought with the world and won your supremacy, after you have dominated the world in your own way, you have to walk along the Road of Eternity to reach perfection in life."

Both the seeker in us and the vital in us then fight against the world and bring the world under their feet. But once they dominate the world, they are satisfied. Then they don't want to walk along the road any farther. They don't want to reach the destined Goal. They forget the promise they made to God that after they enjoyed their supremacy for a while they would walk along the road to reach the highest Truth and Light.

When the mind and the seeker become one, they say to God, "Lord, we shall definitely listen to You. You want us to march on along the road, and we shall do so. But before that, please allow us to think, to judge, to see if the world deserves our faith or our doubt. Let us spend some time either in doubting the world or in having faith in the world, in thinking of ourselves or in thinking of the world. When all this is done, we shall without fail proceed along Eternity's Road. To please You, to fulfill Your Command, we shall without fail reach the highest Height."

God, out of His infinite Bounty, says to the mind and the seeker in us, "Children, all right, I will allow you to fulfill your desire. But don't forget to fulfill My Desire after you have fulfilled your own. You have to go on, go on, go on. You have to walk along Eternity's Road and reach the highest Goal."

So the mind and the seeker within us start thinking of the world day and night. They start doubting the world, and occasionally they exercise their faith in the world. That is enough for them. They become satisfied and totally forget their promise to God. They don't want to go forward anymore. They don't want the highest Truth, the highest Light, the highest Reality, the illumining Perfection and fulfilling Satisfaction. So the body, the vital and the mind fail.

But the seeker in us also has the heart. When the seeker and the heart become friends, they are doubtful in the beginning whether they will be able to obey God's Command to walk along this eternal road. They see that their brothers, the body, the vital and the mind, have totally failed, although they had good intentions. They just wanted to sleep a little; they just wanted to dominate a little; they just wanted to think and doubt a little, and then they were ready to please God in His own Way. But they failed. They did not keep their promises to God.

So the heart and the seeker in us are confused and worried when they start. They say to God, "We want to please You in Your own Way, in spite of knowing that the rest of the members of our family have failed You. We would also like to come to You by doing something."

God says, "What is it?"

The seeker and the heart say, "We wish to identify ourselves with the achievements of the body, vital and mind."

God says, "Their achievements are nothing but frustration and destruction."

The heart says, "We know, but we are tempted to feel their frustration and destruction first, then we will immediately come to You for satisfaction. We will definitely start walking along Eternity's Road, for we desperately need abiding satisfaction."

God says to the heart and the seeker, "All right, My children, you may try."

So the heart becomes one with the body, the vital and the mind. Then the quality of the body, which is lethargy, the quality of the vital, which is aggression or supremacy, the qualities of the mind, which are suspicion and division, all immediately enter into the heart! It was eager to please God in His own Way when it saw the confusion that the body, vital and mind had created by not doing so. But temptation arose in the aspiring human heart, and because of this temptation the heart became one, inseparably one, with the rest of the members of the family before it was in a position to offer its existence totally to the Supreme Pilot, the Captain Supreme.

So the heart and the seeker become helplessly and hopelessly one with the body, vital and mind for some time. But after having known and felt their suffering, dissatisfaction and frustration, the heart starts to cry out for Light and Truth. The body is to some extent satisfied with its achievements. The vital is to some extent satisfied with its achievements. The mind is to some extent satisfied with its achievements. But the heart, fortunately, is not satisfied with its achievements. The heart wants to achieve something higher, something deeper, something more fulfilling and more illumining. So the heart approaches God.

It says to God, "Lord, I am entirely Yours. Now tell me, shall I stay with You and receive Your Light while walking along Eternity's Road, or shall I stay inside the body, the vital and the mind to cry for Your Light? Which do You want? Shall I give up my body-consciousness, shall I give up my vital-consciousness, shall I give up my mind-consciousness in order to please You? Or shall I remain inside them and invoke Your Light? Please tell me."

God says to the heart-seeker, "If you are really brave, if you feel that you can pray and meditate inside the lethargic body, the aggressive vital, the doubtful and suspicious mind, then I have no objection. But it is an almost impossible task. You have to come out of the body-consciousness. You have to come out of the vital-consciousness. You have to come out of the mind-consciousness. First you have to be inundated with boundless light, and only then can you enter the body-consciousness and change its lethargy into alertness and dynamism. Only then can you change the aggression of the vital into a positive will for God-manifestation; only then can you change the mind's doubt and suspicion into constant faith. If you want to please the young members of your family—your body, vital and mind—you have to first become strong and please Me. Heart, if you please Me in My own Way, only then will the rest of the members of your family be pleased."

The heart fully accepts God's Command and wholeheartedly tries to fulfill God's Will; therefore, the heart becomes inseparably one with God's Will, and receives and achieves light in abundant measure. Then God tells the heart to enter into the mind, vital, and body for their illumination, and the heart obeys. It suffers a lot, because the body, vital and mind do not want to accept the heart's light.

But the heart has boundless patience, and this patience is

the lengthening of time itself. Patience is the constant expansion of time within us. So now the seeker and his heart are inundating the seeker's physical body, his vital and his mind with the Light of the Supreme. They are not being compelled to do this by any outer force or by the members of their family; they are acting out of their inseparable inner oneness with the Lord Supreme, who wants them to illumine the younger members of their family. In order to discover perfection in life, what we need is a flood of light and delight within us.

We are all seekers of the infinite Truth. We have to know that what we have principally is the heart and the mind. The mind is constantly bringing us the message of subtraction and division. The heart is constantly bringing us the message of addition and multiplication. It is through addition and multiplication that illumination, salvation, liberation, realization and perfection evolve. Therefore, let us feel from now on that what we have is only the heart. The divine qualities of our heart can not only fulfill the divine in us, but also awaken the stone-consciousness and the plant-consciousness in us, transform the animal in us and illumine the human in us. So let us try to become only the heart, which has the inner longing to fulfill God in all the members of our inner family.

6

Meditation: Language of the Soul

Sri Chinmoy offers the opening meditation at the First Plenary Session of the World Parliament of Religions in Chicago on August 8, 1993. This was the largest and most representative gathering of spiritual and religious leaders in history.

Invitation to Meditate

Our weekly meditations here at the United Nations are not only for the United Nations, but also for the world at large. Our meditations are for the God-lovers and the lovers of humanity. If we really love God, and if we really love mankind and consciously believe that we are responsible for mankind, then we must feel that our aspiration and dedication to the soul of the United Nations and our Inner Pilot is of paramount importance.

Our own aspiration will expedite the vision of the United Nations. And when that vision is transformed into reality, the Inner Pilot will know our contribution, whether or not the world ever recognizes it. Our contribution, which is our aspiration, cannot be measured by money-power or any kind of world-recognition. It can be measured only by God's Love-Power, His Concern-Power and His Satisfaction-Power.

Meditation: Discovery and Invention

What is meditation? Meditation is not a kind of prayer of the mind, and it is not a prayer in the mind. But it can easily serve the purpose of a soulful prayer for the mind.

We meditate for various reasons. Peace of mind we all badly need. Therefore, when we meditate, either consciously or unconsciously we aim for peace of mind. Meditation gives us peace of mind without a tranquilizer, and this peace of mind that we get from meditation does not fade away. It lasts for good in the inmost recesses of our aspiring heart.

Meditation gives us purity. Some people advocate the traditional Indian system of breathing in order to achieve purity. By breathing systematically and also through some occult techniques of breathing, one can definitely purify one's internal system to some extent, but this purity does not last permanently. However, when one prays and meditates soulfully and brings the soul to the fore, one is bound to achieve lasting purity. The purity that we get from our soulful meditation lasts forever in our aspiring consciousness.

When we pray, we feel the mistake-world looming large. Either we have made a mistake by having done something or we have made a mistake by not having done something. Then our sincerity compels us to confess our mistake and ask for forgiveness. Prayer and confession very often go together. But meditation does not believe in that kind of confession. Meditation says, "Why do you have to make a mistake and then confess it? Do not remain near mistakes. Remain millions and billions and trillions of miles away from mistakes. Then you won't have to confess anything."

Meditation is not an escape exercise. When we pray, we try to bring down into us a higher reality, or enter into a higher reality which will separate us from the world of suffering. We try to escape from the suffering of the world. But when we meditate, we do not try to escape. The seeker who meditates is a warrior, a divine warrior. He faces suffering, ignorance and darkness, and inside the very life and breath of suffering he tries to establish the kingdom of wisdom-light.

The true seeker who meditates also knows that whatever he is doing is not for his own personal salvation. If everything that he is doing is only for his own salvation, then he and the world will always remain two different entities with two different ideals or goals. Therefore, sincere seekers always try to assimilate the world-truth, world-light and world-capacity, and meditate for world-transformation, world-illumination and world-perfection.

Real meditation never forces us to do something, to say something or to become something. It is the desiring vital or the desiring mind that sometimes enters into our meditation and instigates us to try to achieve something. But meditation proper will never compel us to do something, to say something or to become something, for it knows that everything has to be natural and spontaneous. It only helps us enter cheerfully into the current of spiritual life.

Human life is beset with difficulties and dangers, but we can overcome these obstacles. We can take each difficulty as a powerful warning, and each danger as a blessing-light in disguise. The meditation-world invites us and leads us to the highest Reality. We see ahead of us a light, which is perfection-light. But as soon as we see this light that can perfect us, we are frustrated. A red traffic light is frustration to us, especially when we are in a hurry to reach our destination. But we forget that it is the red light that saves our precious life from destruction. The red traffic light is regular and punctual. Regularly and punctually it warns us and saves us. Similarly, regularity in meditation saves us, illumines us and fulfills us. The life of our outer smile is strengthened by the regularity of our prayer, and the light of our inner cry is increased by the regularity of our meditation.

When we meditate, we discover something and we invent something. From our regular meditation, we discover faith inside us. This discovery we do not get from anything else. Immense, continuous, illumining and fulfilling faith we get only from our pure and sure meditation. And what do we invent? We invent gratitude. Our heart becomes the possessor of something which it did not possess previously, and that something is boundless gratitude. Each meditation creates a gratitude-flower inside our heart, and petal by petal this flower blossoms in worship of our Beloved Lord Supreme. So we invent gratitude and discover faith from our meditation.

Meditation helps us hear the Voice of God. It not only helps us hear the Voice of God, but it also helps us listen to the Voice of God. After hearing the Voice of God, either we can stop or we can continue further and actually listen to God's Voice. If we listen to the Voice of God, if we listen to the inner dictates at every moment, then the world of confusion that baffles us, and that we ourselves create, will no longer exist for us.

There is a special way to listen to the Voice of God, and that special way is to meditate in silence. Silent meditation is the strongest force that can ever be seen, felt and utilized. How do we meditate silently? Just by not talking, just by not using our mouths, we are not doing silent meditation. Silent meditation is totally different. When we start meditating in silence, we feel the vast calmness of the bottom of the sea within us and around us. The life of activity, movement and restlessness is on the surface, but deep below there is poise and silence. Either we shall imagine this sea of silence within us and around us, or we shall feel that we are nothing but a sea of poise itself.

If we can meditate in this way, we are bound to hear the Voice of God and we are bound to listen to the Voice of God. Once we become accustomed to listening to the Voice of God, we will feel that there is no such thing as the future, there is no such thing even as today; there is only now. God is now; His Vision is now. The eternal Now is the only reality. In the eternal Now we grow and glow; in the eternal Now we please God, fulfill God and become perfect instruments of God.

Meditation: Self-Transcendence

Meditation is self-transcendence. Self-transcendence is the message of the Beyond. The message of the Beyond is God the eternally evolving Soul and God the eternally fulfilling Goal.

The animal in man is proud of his self-aggrandizement. The human in man is delighted with his self-awareness. The divine in man is conscious of his self-realization. The Supreme in man is fulfilled in his self-transcendence.

Man needs material wealth to enjoy a prosperous earthly life. Man needs meditation to live a peaceful Heavenly life. Man needs revelation to live as a divine hero who guides and serves humanity. Heaven does not need a weakling. Earth does not want a weakling.

Life is not mere empty talk. Life is not the breath of illusion. Life is the action of aspiration. Aspiration is the cry of man's soul. Let us fight the battle of life within. Let us wake up to the reality of our world consciously and devotedly. Ours will be the victory without. We must never forget that we are of God the Infinite and we are for God the Eternal

Meditation means the evolution of the body and the soul. The body's ultimate evolution is transformation and perfection. The soul's ultimate evolution is the highest illumination and complete manifestation.

He who meditates consciously dedicates his life to God. He who soulfully dedicates his life to mankind unconsciously meditates on the real God. His are the eyes that see Heaven on earth. In him divinity and humanity are triumphantly blended.

Temptation and meditation. Temptation is precisely what an unaspiring man knows. Meditation is precisely what an aspiring man does. An unaspiring man must descend on the ladder of life and feel the very breath of ignorance. An aspiring man eternally ascends the ladder of life and lives in the very Heart of God.

We have hundreds of secrets, but meditation has only one: competence is achievement. Competence and achievement are the smiles of God's unconditional Grace.

Sri Krishna meditated. He became God, the Love Divine. The Buddha meditated. He became God, the Light Divine. The Christ meditated. He became God, the Compassion Divine. Now God wants you to meditate. He wants you to become God, the Life Divine.

Can Meditation Enhance Leadership?

Can meditation enhance leadership? The answer is definitely affirmative. Meditation can and does enhance leadership. But we have to know what we mean by meditation. If meditation means a secluded life, if meditation means only an individual triumph over self, this type of meditation can never enhance leadership. If meditation means that I exist only for myself, if it means that self-mastery is my only goal and that I alone am important on earth, then leadership cannot be enhanced, for there is no necessity of leadership. If meditation means a secluded life, a life of isolated progress, then the necessity for leadership does not arise at all. If I alone am the focus of all my effort, who am I to lead? Only when there are two or more persons is leadership necessary or important. Either I take the lead or somebody else takes the lead.

If meditation means an expansion of consciousness, if meditation means that we are of all and for all—that we are of our inner divinity and for aspiring humanity—then our qualities of leadership are bound to increase. The light of meditation will make these qualities grow from bright to brighter and from brighter to brightest. The light of meditation will transform much into more and more into most.

When we encounter leadership, immediately the physical in us surrenders because it is perfectly aware of its teeming limitations. It knows how weak and frail it is, how insignificant its capacity is. But the vital in us immediately sees leadership as a kind of challenge either from the inner world or from the outer world. After accepting the challenge, the vital wants to conquer and dominate the world around it. The vital immediately wants to dominate others, to kick the world around like a football for its own pleasure. This is the vital's idea of leadership.

Mental leadership is somewhat different. In mental leadership we notice that the world around us is all imperfection, and we feel that only our own mental world is perfect. Since we feel that we are perfect and everybody else is imperfect, we try to lead others in order to perfect them. But as long as we see only imperfection around us and feel that our being alone is flooded with perfection and light, then we are not the right instrument to lead others.

There is another type of leadership called psychic leadership; leadership of the heart. This leadership is totally different from vital and mental leadership. Psychic leadership is founded upon the heart's inner awareness and oneness with reality as a whole. Whoever leads from the heart is a real leader. This is not the leadership of a self-appointed leader. This leadership is the recognition of our own inseparable oneness with the rest of humanity. The one is for the many and the many are for the one. When we think of ourselves as the one, we feel that we are like the trunk of the tree, and the many are our branches, leaves, flowers and fruits. When we think of ourselves as the many, as the branches, leaves, flowers and fruits, we also feel that we are part of the trunk. Here real oneness makes us feel that all are equally responsible for embodying the highest Truth, revealing the highest Truth and manifesting the highest Truth.

Meditation is a dynamic, active power; it is movement. Movement itself is progress. Movement itself is the growth and expansion of our reality. Whenever we meditate, no matter what plane of consciousness we are on, at that time we are moving towards some destination which we are eventually going to reach. While progressing towards the destination, this movement increases its potentiality, its capacity, its reality, its vision, its identity with its Source. Once it reaches the Source, all its capacities increase in boundless measure.

In the outer world, a leader is he who has more capacity or more opportunity than other individuals. If his capacity far surpasses theirs, then he becomes the leader. But in the spiritual life, it is not like that. In the spiritual life, real leadership depends on one's awareness of reality and one's conscious and constant acceptance of this reality as one's very own. If one can accept the reality around him as his very own despite all its imperfection, limitation and bondage, then he is the real leader, not he who has a little more capacity than another individual or the rest of the group.

He who claims his brothers and sisters as his very own, he who accepts the challenge of ignorance and who stands in front of ignorance-night determined to conquer it and transform it into the flood of light—he is the real leader. In the spiritual life, leadership means our conscious wish to be a chosen instrument of the Supreme. The moment we become His chosen instrument, we become real leaders. A divine instrument is he who has the capacity to lead and guide humanity.

According to Indian scripture, when a devotee worships the cosmic gods and goddesses, the capacity of the gods and goddesses increases. You may ask how this can be. The cosmic gods and goddesses already have tremendous peace, light and bliss. Just from the worship of a devotee, how can these qualities increase? It is like saying that if you stand in front of the ocean and worship the ocean, immediately the length and breadth of the ocean will increase. Your physical mind will immediately laugh at the idea, but the Indian scriptures were not an inch away from the truth.

What actually increases in the cosmic gods and goddesses when they are worshiped is their conscious awareness of humanity's need for them. When the gods feel that they are consciously needed by humanity as a whole, they feel they have a task to perform on earth. They think, "The children of earth need us. Let us help them, let us guide them, let us mold them, let us shape them into divine beings." When the cosmic gods and goddesses feel earth's need, immediately they shower their choicest blessings on earth. The satisfaction that dawns in them because of earth's need is the increase of their capacity. Previously earth did not need them, humanity did not need them; so their capacities remained dormant. But when they are pleased and satisfied with humanity, they deliberately bring forward and increase all their capacities.

We are spiritual people; we need peace, light and bliss in abundant measure. That is why we invoke the presence of the cosmic gods. But there are people who want divine help in order to achieve something which will not be a creative force at all, but rather, a destructive force. Indian mythology offers us hundreds of stories about seekers who meditate for years and years and, at the close of their journey, when their chosen deity is satisfied and agrees to grant them a boon, they ask for something destructive. One very well-known story is about a devotee of Lord Shiva who meditated for years and years to satisfy Lord Shiva. Then the boon he asked for was this: that any person whose head he touched would immediately be burned to ashes. When Shiva granted him this boon, he wanted to test it on Shiva's head. Shiva ran away and took shelter with Vishnu, another cosmic god. Eventually Vishnu's clever wisdom saved Shiva. Vishnu said to the aspirant, "You are a fool. Why do you have to chase Shiva in order to know whether the boon is genuine? You could easily place your hand on your own head and see its efficacy." The foolish aspirant did this and was himself immediately burned to ashes.

What do we learn from this story? When we cry for something undivine or destructive, the boon may be granted, but there is a divine force which is infinitely more powerful than our undivine force, and this will come to God's aid. If God does not fulfill our ignorance-prayer, it is a real blessing. When He does fulfill our ignorance-prayer in order to give us an experience, then we have to know that this experience is necessary so that we will learn to cry for real Truth and Light. After giving us the necessary experience of ignorance, God will try to pull us towards His Height. At that time He does not actually destroy the capacity of our prayer; He only shows us that the capacity of our prayer should be directed towards a higher goal.

In India, when thieves are about to commit a theft, first they pray to the goddess Kali so that they will not be caught red-handed. Mother Kali may listen to them a few times, but after a while they are caught. When they pray, Mother Kali says, "All right, if you want a life of ignorance, I will fulfill your ignorance." But there comes a time when her higher wisdom, which is compassion, starts to operate. She wants these desire-bound souls to be liberated from ignorance, so she exposes them to earthly justice.

If we want to achieve leadership through the fulfillment of ignorance, God may grant us that boon. But when we have the inner cry, God immediately removes from us the leadership which is based on ignorance and kindles the flame of aspiration in us, so that we can become endowed with divine leadership and be the torch-bearers of His Light and Truth.

On the physical plane, we have a human body. When the physical in us listens to the inner voice or has free access to the inner being, even the physical can become a real leader. All of you know of India's great political leader, the father of the Indian renaissance, Mahatma Gandhi. His physical frame was very frail and weak, but his physical frame embodied inner light in abundant measure. His mental capacity may not have been on the same level with that of Nehru and others, but his soul's light guided India's fate, and the leaders who were mental giants sat at his feet. Why? Just because he saw a higher light, a higher truth, which he wanted to express through his philosophy of *ahimsa*, or non-violence. *Ahimsa* does not mean that one will not strike someone or fight with someone. The vision that Gandhi's non-violence embodied and wanted to reveal was the vision of universal and transcendental Light in humanity. That is why he became India's unparalleled and supreme leader. A real leader is he who has inner light in boundless measure; it is he who represents the soul, he who wants to convey the message of the soul.

It is said that a poet is born, not made. There is much truth in this. But I have seen that by the grace of spiritual masters, or by the grace of inner awakening, many people have become poets. I am using the word in its largest sense, to mean an artist in any plane of consciousness or in any form of art. If one has not brought with him at birth a particular capacity, that does not mean he will not be able to acquire or develop that capacity in this lifetime. If one has not come into the world with the quality of leadership, it does not mean that person will never be able to learn leadership in this incarnation. No! If one accepts the spiritual life, it means one is beginning a new life. If one has an inner guide, a spiritual master, he enters into a new life and is awakened to the highest Truth. A new life means a new hope, a new promise, a new prophecy, a new dream which is about to blossom into reality. This new life is bound to offer the seeker what he needs, whether it be leadership or anything else.

An individual can become a divine instrument even though he did not originally bring down that quality. Everyone has the capacity to be a divine instrument. To become a chosen instrument of God is to become a divine leader. This can be done by mutual acceptance. If light accepts darkness as its very own, and if night accepts light as its very own—that is to say, if the higher part in us is accepted by the lower part and vice versa—only then can the light act in and through the darkness, which needs guidance and constant assurance. If he who needs and he who has can consciously become one, then each one sees and acts through the other. The lowest needs the highest for its realization. The highest needs the lowest for its manifestation.

The capacity for leadership is not the sole monopoly of any individual. It is granted to all. But each individual has to be aware that this capacity and reality abide in him. He has to exercise his inner capacity; he has to feel the need of this reality. Then automatically, spontaneously, divine leadership comes forward and increases in boundless measure. How does it come to the fore? This occurs when one consciously and constantly feels that he is of one Source and for all mankind. This moment he is the Creator; the next moment he is the creation. When he thinks of himself as the Creator, he is one. When he thinks of himself as the creation, he is many. He has to see and become the Dream; he has to see and become the Reality; and finally, he has to see the Dream and the Reality in his being as one, each complementing the other. Dream we need to fly in the sky of the ever-transcending Beyond. Reality we need to manifest the transcendental Height and to give value to the universality in and around us. The song of the Transcendental we sing through our Dream. The song of the Universal we sing through our Reality. Both Transcendental and Universal, both Dream and Reality make us whole, complete and perfect.

Mediation and Meditation

Two conflicting parties need to reach a compromise. A third party, the mediator, is then of paramount importance. His is the task of offering light to the conflicting and strangling parties. When the mediator is successful, the two conflicting parties end their mutual hostility. They live—or at least try to live—peacefully, in their own domain.

The animal in us incites us by roaring that might is right. The human in us inspires us by feeling deep within that right is might. The divine in us illumines us by offering the supreme truth that it is God alone who has all Might and who is all Right.

When we look at the unlit consciousness found on the human level, we see something quite disappointing and damaging. We see that this unlit consciousness is very often unthinking, unaspiring and possessive. But if we invoke the Grace of God, the divine Grace can transform the unthinking consciousness into the thinking, the unaspiring consciousness into the aspiring and the possessive consciousness into the renouncing.

Here on earth, where everything is fleeting, if we can derive a little joy, a little peace, a little harmony from our mental wisdom, we should be proud of this achievement. At a certain stage in human development, when most of the people are not aspiring to become perfect, mediation is of great importance. Therefore, we must pay reverential attention to mediation. It is a temporary mental relief, a pause, a rest in the life of constant conflict. It is a clever compromise. But to expect abiding peace and illumining fulfillment from mediation is simply absurd. We cannot expect lasting peace and we must not expect illumining fulfillment from mediation. For these higher goals we need meditation.

The United Nations is the mediator unmatched and unparalleled in today's world. Its achievements are unique in the physical world, the vital world, the mental world and the psychic world. Unfortunately, these achievements do not or cannot last, because they are human achievements, not divine achievements.

Very often, animal aggression gives birth to human self-aggrandizement. This human self-aggrandizement is chased by bitter frustration. Later on, human aggrandizement is devoured by utter destruction.

In the spiritual life, in our inner life, we also see two conflicting parties: fear and doubt on one side, and inner courage and faith on the other side. Meditation plays two distinctive roles in the inner life. Meditation is the medicine, the ultimate cure for our fear and our doubt. It transforms our fear into strength, into adamantine will. It transforms our doubt into constant, unmistakable and inevitable certainty. Again, we see that meditation is the road and the guide to the Goal. He who is surcharged with inner courage and faith will get constant help and illumination from meditation as he walks, marches and runs along the road to his ultimate Goal.

In the outer world, the blind human body needs constant mediation. The unlit human vital needs striking mediation. The unclear human mind needs illumining mediation. The weak human heart needs lasting mediation.

In the inner world, the fleeting, unaspiring human body needs constant meditation. The running, struggling vital needs striking meditation. The searching and climbing human mind needs illumining meditation. The crying and aspiring human heart needs everlasting meditation.

In the outer world of turmoil, mediation is necessary. In the inner world of frustration and despair, meditation is necessary. If we can bring the result of meditation to the fore from the inner world, then mediation in the outer world will have a new life that will be flooded with everlasting peace, light and bliss. In the fleeting, in the finite, we shall hear the message of the Eternal and the Infinite.

Does Meditation Really Accomplish Anything?

First of all, let us try to know and understand what meditation actually means. What is meditation? Meditation is man's inner movement and outer progress. Meditation is man's inner soulful promise and outer fruitful manifestation.

A man of no aspiration will dauntlessly ask, "Does meditation really accomplish anything?" A man of sterling faith and aspiration will confidently ask, "Is there anything on earth, in God's creation, that meditation cannot accomplish? Is there anything that cannot be achieved by meditation?"

God will immediately answer these two questions. To the man who has no aspiration, God will say, "My child, sleep, sleep. You need rest." To the one who is all aspiration, God will say, "My child, fly, fly! My highest Height of the transcendental Beyond is eagerly expecting your arrival."

What is the first and foremost thing we expect from meditation? Peace. Peace and nothing else. Meditation is the embodiment of peace. The present-day world needs only one thing: peace.

The great peace-lover, former Secretary-General Dag Hammarskjöld, offers us a sublime message: "No peace which is not peace for all. . . ." In peace, what looms large is eternal, fulfilling rest. He says, ". . . no rest until all has been fulfilled."

Why do we meditate? We meditate just because our life needs inspiration, our life needs aspiration. Aspiration is, to some extent, a form of meditation. It is our meditation that promises to give us our realization-tree. Today meditation plays the role of aspiration, and tomorrow meditation will play the role of realization. The Inner Pilot, the Pilot Supreme within us, inspires us to act; it is He who has already kept the fruit of action safe in the life of our aspiration.

The truth-seeker in Dag Hammarskjöld, on the strength of his own inner conviction, said, "Somebody placed the shuttle in your hand: somebody who had already arranged the threads."

In our human life two things are of paramount importance: role and goal. At every moment we have to know what our role in life is, and we also have to be conscious that we have a goal. At our journey's start we have to become fully aware of our role, and at our journey's close we have to be fully conscious of our ultimate Goal. Meditation is this connecting link between our role in the Divine Play and our ultimate Goal in God's ever-evolving universe. Man's role is his conscious self-surrender to the Will of the Absolute Supreme. Man's Goal, the Goal of Goals, is his constant self-surrender to the absolute Will of the Supreme.

Life is conscious ascent and conscious descent. When we say ascent, what do we actually mean? We mean life's aspiration ascending towards the Highest. When we say descent, we mean the illumining descent of the soul's all-transforming and all-fulfilling meditation. The individual human life is an ascending prayer. Again, the divine soul in each human being is a descending meditation. The ascending cry and the descending Grace are inseparable. Together they fulfill the Absolute here on earth.

As human beings are countless, even so are their endless prayers. Each human being can doubt the value of spiritual prayer during this short span of life, but no human being on earth can say that he has never prayed. Be it for a fleeting second or for hours or for months or for years, each individual has prayed. This prayer has intrinsic value. And just as one individual can far surpass the rest of mankind similarly, one particular prayer far surpasses all other prayers.

The profound seeker in Dag Hammarskjöld offers an unparalleled prayer for mankind:

Before Thee in humility,
With Thee in faith:
In Thee in peace.

This prayer asks for nothing but offers everything.

Does meditation accomplish anything? Meditation does accomplish something; in fact, it accomplishes everything. God's Divinity meditated and created humanity, humanity in infinite shapes and forms. God's humanity meditates, and before long we shall see the result: the sun of perfect Perfection will shine on the face of aspiring humanity.

Here we are all seekers of the infinite Truth. None of us has even an iota of doubt about the efficacy of meditation. But we have friends, neighbors, acquaintances who may ask us, "Does meditation really accomplish anything?" We can tell them, "O unbelievers, O disbelievers, do not sit on the unsure ground of doubt. Look. Here is the key: meditation. Meditation is the key to unlocking the door of God's Plenitude and Infinitude. Before you entered into the world-arena, yours was the promise to realize Him here in this body, Him to fulfill, Him to manifest here on earth. Now spread your meditation-wings once and for all, and catch the first morning breeze with your soul's Soulful promise to the Absolute Supreme."

Prayer-Life, Meditation-Life, Contemplation-Life

Why do we pray? We pray because we want to become great. We pray because we want to become good. When we become great, we feel that the entire world is at our feet, that the entire world is at our command. When we become good, we feel that the entire world is in us and that the entire world is for us.

By praying we can become either another Julius Caesar or Napoleon, or another Christ or Krishna. When we become a Caesar or Napoleon, we will try to conquer the world to serve ourselves. But when we become another Christ or Krishna, we will plead with the world to grant us the opportunity to elevate and illumine the world-consciousness. We will make other human beings feel that ours is the task to serve and fulfill them the way the Eternal Beloved Supreme wants to fulfill them.

A life of prayer is a life of simplicity. Simplicity is a very common word, but it houses the highest Truth. God is all simplicity. When we are simple, we come to realize that there are very few things that we actually need. Each time we can eliminate one need from our list of necessities, we gain an iota of peace of mind. And it is peace of mind that is of paramount importance in our earthly life.

Right after simplicity we see that there is something else. This is a friend, a real friend, who is waiting for us and welcoming us. The name of that friend is sincerity. When we become sincere, we are bound to feel that our goal can be reached, that the goal need not and cannot remain always a far cry. The life of sincerity makes us feel that we are eternal travelers along the Road of Eternity. Today's goal, as we reach it, becomes the starting point for tomorrow's new adventure. We are in the process of progressing towards an ever-transcending Goal, an ever-transcending Reality.

Then comes the life of purity. Each time we pray, we feel that something within us is coming to the fore, and that "something" is purity. This purity-friend of ours is liked most by our Eternal Father, our Beloved Supreme. Our Eternal Father feels that His Vision, His Dream, His Reality—whatever He has and whatever He is—can be expressed, revealed and manifested most soulfully, divinely and supremely through purity. A breath of purity holds God the Infinite, God the Eternal and God the Immortal.

Each prayer leads us to an experience. This experience can at times make us feel how helpless we are in comparison with infinite Light and Delight. Again, this experience can make us feel that Infinity, Eternity and Immortality are not vague terms, but real realities within our easy reach.

After we have had the experience of the reality, we go one step farther: we knock at the door of realization. When we enter into the room of realization, we see that the things we wanted to achieve, the things we have spent years or even incarnations trying to achieve, are already within us. For Eternity they have been within us, only we did not have the vision to see them. Now we not only see them, but also claim them as our very own.

Each individual here is a seeker. That means each of us has a prayer within us and also something else, which is called meditation. When we are in the prayer-world, each time we think of our body, our physical consciousness, we are reminded of something else, something more fulfilling. When we think of our physical consciousness, our earthly frame, we feel that we need something else to satisfy ourselves and to satisfy the needs of the rest of the world. But when we dive deep within and establish a free access to our inner life of meditation, we see that we have everything; we only have to offer it and distribute it to others. When we consider ourselves as the soul, as the divine representative of God, the highest absolute

Truth, then we see, we feel and we know clearly that we have everything within us; only we have to reveal it and offer it to the world at large.

When we look at the United Nations Secretariat building from the outside, when we look at the body of the United Nations, we feel that the United Nations is like a beggar: it needs everything in God's creation. A beggar needs everything for himself, not for anybody else. His is an unquenchable thirst. But once we are inside the Secretariat building, we feel the infinite light, peace and harmony that is inside the soul of the United Nations. This soul is crying at every moment to be of service to mankind. If we can become one with the soul of the United Nations, then we see that it has everything: world-peace, world-harmony, world-union, world-oneness.

This is the case not only with the United Nations, but also with each human being. Each time we pray with the body, in the body, for the body, we have to feel that we are acting like beggars. We feel that there is something outside us that we need in order to satisfy ourselves. But if we remain in the soul-consciousness, in our inner life, then we become real emperors: we know and feel that we have everything.

Of course, there is a difference between a human emperor and a divine emperor. When a human emperor gives something to his subjects, he feels a sense of gratification. He feels that his subjects are at his mercy. They depend on his boundless compassion. But the divine emperor feels that each human being on earth is part and parcel of his own existence. He is composed, like the ocean, of thousands of drops. Each drop is equally necessary. When he does something for an individual being, or for all of mankind, he feels that he is only pleasing, satisfying and fulfilling his own dream, which is blossoming like a lotus, petal by petal.

The body reminds us of the necessity of prayer. The soul reminds us of the necessity of meditation. Each time we pray, we feel that the finite consciously or unconsciously is trying to enter into the Infinite. Each time we meditate, we feel that we are cheerfully, devotedly and soulfully welcoming the Infinite to manifest itself in and through us. But there is something more: a living reality which we call contemplation.

In our prayer-life we go up to see, to feel, to bring down something. In our meditation-life we go deep within and open ourselves to become the recipient, so that in and through us the highest Reality can manifest itself. But in contemplation we embody both earth-consciousness and Heaven-consciousness. We embody the divine lover and the Eternal Beloved. We embody the finite and the Infinite. When we contemplate, we feel that the finite and the Infinite are interdependent. The finite needs the Infinite; the Infinite needs the finite. Earth needs Heaven; Heaven needs earth. The divine lover needs the Supreme Beloved; the Beloved Supreme needs the lover divine.

When we want to sing the song of the many in the One, we embody the Heaven-consciousness, the Infinite and the Supreme Beloved. When we want to play the role of the One in the many, we embody the earth-consciousness, the finite and the divine lover. Each individual will ultimately be able to feel that one moment he is the trunk of the tree of the one absolute Reality, and the next moment he is the branches and the countless leaves, flowers and fruits. Each seeker embodies and each seeker at every moment has the boundless duty to fulfill God the Creator and God the creation. This duty he fulfills only when he feels that he is of the One and for the many, as well as of the many and for the One.

When the seeker identifies himself inseparably with the earth-consciousness, he feels that there is a constant hunger in him, a hunger that constantly mounts high, higher, highest. When he identifies himself with the Heaven-consciousness, he feels there is constant nourishment, boundless energy and infinite nectar-delight in him; he feels that Immortality is growing in and through him. The seeker who has learned contemplation is at once infinite hunger and infinite delight. In the body-consciousness he needs. In the soul-consciousness he not only has, but also he eternally is.

Experiencing Concentration, Meditation and Contemplation

Concentration, meditation and contemplation are of utmost importance in the spiritual life. Therefore, let us try to concentrate, meditate and contemplate. First we shall concentrate.

I have offered to each of you a flower. Try to look at the entire flower for a few seconds. While you are looking at the entire flower, please feel that you are the flower and also that this flower is growing inside the inmost recesses of your heart. You are the flower and, at the same time, you are growing inside your own heart. Then gradually try to concentrate on one particular petal, any petal that you select. Feel that the petal is the seed-form of your reality-existence. After a few minutes' time, concentrate again on the entire flower, and feel that this flower is the universal reality. In this way go back and forth. Keep your eyes half open and do not allow any thought to enter into your mind. Try to make your mind absolutely calm, quiet and tranquil.

Now close your eyes and try to see the flower that you have concentrated upon inside your heart. Then, in the same way you did with your eyes open, concentrate on the flower inside your heart with your eyes closed.

Now we shall meditate. Keep your eyes half open and imagine the vast sky. Either try to see or feel the vast sky right in front of you. In the beginning, try to feel that the sky is in front of you; then later, try to feel that you are as vast as the sky, or that you are the vast sky itself.

Now close your eyes and feel that you are the Universal Heart. Try to see and feel the vast sky inside your heart. You are the Universal Heart, and inside you is the sky that you meditated upon and identified yourself with. The Universal

Heart is infinitely, infinitely vaster than the sky, so you can easily house the sky within yourself.

Now we shall contemplate. Kindly try to imagine a golden being which is infinitely more beautiful than the most beautiful child that you have ever seen on earth. This being is your Beloved Lord Supreme. You are all divine God-lovers, supreme God-lovers, and the golden being is your Beloved Lord Supreme.

Now with your eyes half open in the beginning, please try to feel both your existence and the presence of your Supreme Beloved Lord at the top of the highest mountain or at the very bottom of the ocean, whichever is easier for you. After you have felt this, feel that you are the Beloved Supreme and that the golden being is the divine lover. This is like a divine game of hide-and-seek. When you become the Supreme Beloved, the divine lover seeks you. When you become the divine lover, you seek the Supreme Beloved. At one moment you are the divine lover, and the next moment you are the Supreme Beloved Lord. This is contemplation.

The Power of Meditation

Meditation illumines our mind. Meditation purifies our heart. Meditation transforms our life. Meditation satisfies our Inner Pilot, the Lord Supreme—God the One in us, God the many for us, God the transcendental Height and God the universal Breadth.

He who meditates soulfully can easily solve not only his own personal problems, but also all the world's problems, for man the question will always be answered by God the ever-ready Answer.

God asks us to meditate so that at every moment we can claim Him as our own, very own. Once we claim Him as our own, very own, this world of turmoil, unrest, fear, anxiety and worry can and will be conquered. All negative, destructive forces will be conquered through the omnipotent power of our soulful God-dedication-meditation.

The Voice of Silence

No matter how long I speak about the Voice of Silence, I shall not be able to make you hear the Voice of Silence. But I wish to assure you that if you meditate with me for a few minutes before I speak, if you can dive deep within as I shall dive deep within for a few minutes, then either you will hear the Voice of Silence or your prayer and meditation will expedite your journey towards receiving the message of the Voice of Silence.

It is true that it takes years for a seeker to hear the message of the Voice of Silence. But with all my soul's love, I wish to say that on the strength of our inner aspiration and outer dedication to the life divine, we can and will hear the Voice of Silence, which sempiternally is guiding our life. Our outer life—the life of hustle and bustle—either does not hear this voice or, when it does hear it, pays no attention to it. The life of temptation is what our outer life wants, not the life of true fulfillment and satisfaction. The Voice of Silence has the answer when we want divine satisfaction in our day-to-day existence.

The Voice of Silence is the dream of
    God's ever-climbing Aspiration-Dawn.
The Voice of Silence is the reality of
    God's ever-illumining Revelation-Light.
The Voice of Silence is the immortality of
    God's ever-fulfilling Perfection-Height.

What is voice?
Voice is our inner and outer choice.
Hunger for life-destruction is our animal choice.

> Hunger for supremacy-satisfaction is our human choice.
> Hunger for perfection-manifestation
>   is our divine choice.

We wish to hear the Voice of Silence, but how? There are two principal ways. One way is to silence the human mind totally. From the gross physical mind we enter into the intellectual mind. From the intellectual mind we enter into the intuitive mind. From the intuitive mind we enter into the illumined mind. And from the illumined mind we enter into the overmind. It is only from this highest mind that we can expect to hear the message of the Voice of Silence.

The other way is to feel that our heart-vessel has to be filled with divine peace, light, bliss and power. When we want to hear the Voice of Silence through the mind, we empty the mind. But when we want to hear the Voice of Silence through the heart, we fill up the heart. When we empty the mind, we have to know that we do so precisely because we want to be able to receive God the Guest or God the infinite Peace. When we fill up the heart, we feel that God the immortal Light and infinite Delight is entering into our earthly home. The light of the soul precedes the Voice of Silence. The Voice of Silence can never come to the fore unless and until the light of the soul brings it forward consciously, compassionately and lovingly.

What else must we do to hear the Voice of Silence? When we pray, when we meditate, we have to do something quite specific. When we breathe in, we have to imagine consciously that inside that breath, within us, is a peaceful nest and a bird. After a few minutes we have to feel that the nest is our outer existence and the bird our inner existence. Now, this bird has to come out of its nest. How do we bring the bird out of the nest? There are two ways. One way is to make our concentration, meditation and contemplation as dynamic as possible. Here, dynamism means the constant feeling within you of a speeding train that does not stop—an express train that does not stop at any station or at any junction. It is a tireless train, an endless train, continuously going on. When we have that inner feeling, from the very starting point we get the Blessing-Power of the Supreme. In the flow of dynamism, we see the bird of our inner being leaving its nest, and the Supreme gives us the experience of the Voice of Silence.

Another way to hear the Voice of Silence is to feel, the moment you enter into your meditation or start praying, that you are an infinite expanse of ocean. A few minutes later, feel that you are deep inside the ocean, and from there try to spread the wings of the bird that you were when you followed the dynamic way of hearing the Voice of Silence.

A seeker may hear the Voice of Silence as something very faint and feeble—a tiny voice like a ripple on calm water. But this voice, this faint voice, can be compared to an atom. When we split the atom, we release unbelievable power. Similarly, when we know how to hear the Voice of Silence properly, our inner being immediately is inundated with the power of thousands of inner suns. The creation and the Creator immediately come to satisfy us. Once we hear the Voice of Silence consciously in our spiritual life, we feel that, like God, we too are responsible for the entire creation. Like God, it is we who are the Creator and we who are the creation itself.

How can we know whether we are hearing the Voice of Silence or something totally different which we are mistakenly calling the Voice of Silence? We can easily know if it is the Voice of Silence or not. When we hear a voice from the very depths, from the inmost recesses of our heart, and if that voice gives us a message which our outer mind or physical consciousness is ready to accept with utmost joy and love, then we will know that this is the Voice of Silence. If the physical mind or the outer consciousness does not get immediate joy, then it is not the Voice of Silence.

Right now, our outer mind gets joy both in the acceptance of reality and in the rejection of reality. But when the Inner Voice enters into the outer mind, the outer mind has no choice. It immediately accepts the reality as reality. When the Voice of Silence is heard, the outer mind will accept it so wholeheartedly that it will feel the lofty truth it has discovered is its own achievement.

God expresses Himself through both silence and sound. Silence is His Reality's Height; silence is His Reality's Depth. Sound is His Reality's Length; sound is His Reality's Breadth. In silence, God is all assurance. In sound, God is all confidence. In self-assurance, God builds the Kingdom of Light. In self-confidence, God invites His unlit, obscure, unaspiring creation to enter into His Kingdom of Light. A seeker who is a child in the spiritual life finds it quite easy to appreciate, admire and adore God's Length and Breadth. But a seeker who is advanced in the spiritual life inwardly feels that God's Height and God's Depth must be appreciated first; only then can His Length and Breadth be truly and properly appreciated, admired and adored.

The Voice of Silence is God's conscious preparation in man. The Voice of Silence is God's conscious Dream of perfection in man. The Voice of Silence finally becomes God's own ever-transcending, dream-bound Reality and Reality-freed Dream.

O Voice of Silence,
Where are you?
I need your golden wings.
O Voice of God,
Where are You?
Hide not from me.

Meditation: Bridging Heaven and Earth

Meditation is self-perfection. If we have the message of perfection deep within, we cannot neglect any imperfection within us. If we have doubt, we have to transform this doubt into certainty. If we have insecurity, we have to transform this insecurity into confidence. Anything undivine within us must be transformed into something divine. If our eyes see well but our arms and legs are weak, then we are not perfect. We have to strengthen all our limbs and organs and make ourselves integrally perfect.

Some people are afraid of meditation; they feel it is something strange or abnormal. They feel that since everyone does not meditate, that means meditation is something unnatural or useless. But we have to know that just because many people are not doing something, it does not mean that the thing is wrong. Numbers have no value; what matters is our awareness of Truth, Light, Divinity, Infinity, Eternity and Immortality within.

Just the other day an amusing incident took place in front of my house. A neighbor came up to me in a very friendly way and said, "I saw a light in your room at around five o'clock this morning. Usually I don't get up at that time, but today I had to leave early to visit a friend. What were you doing at that hour?" I said to him, "I was meditating. As a matter of fact, I get up every morning at two o'clock to meditate." As soon as I said that, he immediately became disturbed. "Meditation? What is that?" he said. "I don't understand all that. I don't care for it! I don't need it!" Then he quickly left. He was quite upset when he heard that I had been meditating. The very word made him shudder. If I had told him I was reading some interesting novel or watching television, then his friendly attitude would have continued for a long time.

In this world there are many, many people who, like my neighbor, are afraid of meditation. They feel that meditation is something that will take them away from the reality they are familiar with. For them the only reality is the desire-world. If desire goes away, then they have nothing to cling to, nothing to possess and claim as their very own. If they are not playing the game of temptation and becoming victims to temptation, if they are not wallowing in the pleasures of ignorance, then they feel there is no life in what they are doing. For them, life is conscious participation in ignorance, but they call it knowledge, experience, enjoyment.

Our Divine Father has two homes: one is Heaven and the other is earth. In our Heaven-home we enjoy divine rest, and in our earth-home we work and accomplish our multifarious tasks. We have as much right to stay in one home as in the other. When we are in our earth-home, if we act like a stranger and feel that we have come to a place that does not belong to us, then naturally we will want to escape. But why should we have to escape from our own home? Even if we quarrel and fight with the members of our family, still we remain in our home and do not go elsewhere because that home belongs to us. Meditation does not encourage us to escape from reality. Who escapes? He who has done something wrong or he who does not claim reality as his very own.

In the ordinary life there are some people who are fond of watching baseball, volleyball, basketball and other sports, but they do not want to participate. They feel that if they participate, they may not do well or they may be injured, but they do enjoy seeing others play. There are also people who both appreciate watching sports and enjoy participating in them. These people feel that they can feed their cheerfulness and enthusiasm, bring cosmic energy into their system and, at the same time, discard their undivine qualities by participating. In the spiritual life also, there are seekers who want to enjoy the cosmic Game from a distance but do not want to participate actively in this Game. They want to enter into the Himalayan caves or go off to some secluded place to meditate. They are afraid that if they mix with the world, they will lose everything or will not be able to make any progress. But real spirituality is for those who are brave divine soldiers. Thousands of years ago, the Upanishadic seers and the Vedic seers declared: *Nayam atma balahinena labhya*—"The soul cannot be won by the weakling." Only the brave can and will realize the soul.

Also, we have to know that the outer world is not our only enemy. Even if we enter into the Himalayan caves, we still have to deal with our own mind. When we go off by ourselves, the mind plays its role most powerfully. All the world's activities enter into our mind and prevent us from meditating. The mind will start thinking of friends, enemies and various incidents that occurred in our life. So who is the real enemy? We thought our enemy was someone or something outside of us which was disturbing our meditation. But even when we isolate ourselves, we still have to face the mind with all its undivine qualities, and we find that our real enemy is inside us. If we do not conquer the mind and discipline it here amidst the teeming activities of life, there is no guarantee that we will be free from earthly disturbances when we withdraw from the world.

India's greatest poet, Tagore, once made up his mind to go to a lonely forest to compose some songs. He said to himself, "Here I have so much to do, and so many people are constantly bothering me. Yet in spite of this I have written quite a few most significant poems. If I enter into the forest, where I will be all alone, I will be able to write a great many most beautiful poems, many more than I write usually." But after a fortnight in the forest he came back with very little to show for his time, for his mind had been constantly thinking of Shantiniketan, his school, and of his students, his friends and his relatives. He could hardly write at all.

What is reality? Reality is something divine. Reality and Divinity are synonymous, and Divinity and Immortality are synonymous. If something is divine, then it has an immortal life. Here on earth we are crying to be immortal. If we can live on earth for five minutes more, we try to stay. It is very easy for us to say we are not afraid of death, but when we are hurt or when some calamity is taking place, immediately we are afraid that we will die. Those who follow the spiritual life try to conquer death—not in order to live for 200, 300 or 400 years, but in order to have time to accomplish quite a few significant things for Mother-Earth.

While in the soul's world, before entering into a physical body, each person's soul consciously, devotedly and unconditionally makes a solemn promise to the Supreme that here on earth it will manifest its divinity in boundless measure. But once it is inside the physical, in order for the soul to manifest the Supreme on earth, time is necessary. We have to pray, we have to meditate, we have to discipline our life for a long time before we are able to achieve something significant and fulfill our promise to the Almighty Supreme.

If we are able to meditate for only ten years and gain only an iota of peace, light and bliss, with this insignificant quantity of peace, light and bliss, what will we be able to offer to mankind? But if we continue to pray and meditate most soulfully for many years, one day our inner being will be inundated with these divine qualities, and then we will be able to share them abundantly with all and sundry. We accept earth as reality, as divine reality. With our naked eyes we see tremendous aggression, hostility, brutality and other undivine things on earth, but with our inner heart we can feel that this is not the ultimate aim of God. On the contrary, the Vision of God is peace, light and bliss.

We have to know that the creator is always superior to the creation. It is human beings who have created atom bombs and hydrogen bombs. In these people the human mind has reached a high level of development. If the soul's will can now come to the fore and operate in the mind, it will ask the person who has created the atom bomb what he really wants. Immediately his vital will say he wants to conquer. But his soul will reply, "You will not get any satisfaction if you conquer by force, for you will conquer only the body of the world and not the soul. If you do not conquer the soul, then you have conquered nothing. If you really want to establish your victory permanently, then use another kind of power—your soul-power, your love-power, your heart-power."

Reality means the acceptance of life. Reality can never be found in destruction or in domination. Reality is to be found in equality. Reality is in the feeling of inseparable oneness. Does meditation encourage us to escape from reality? No! On the contrary, meditation inspires us to accept God's creation as an unmistakable reality that still awaits transformation and perfection. When our earth-consciousness is transformed, when our own body-consciousness is transformed, only then can we be true receptacles of the infinite Truth and infinite Light.

Earth and each individual on earth must cooperate; otherwise, God's Peace, Light and Bliss will not be received here. Right now, human beings are not able to receive God's Blessings because there is a constant sense of separation between the earth-consciousness and the individual consciousness. But when the earth-consciousness and the individual consciousness unite, earth will play the role of a home, and every human being will play the role of a conscious dweller in the home. What is the use of having a home if there is no dweller? Again, what is the use of having a dweller if there is no home for him to live in?

The earth-home and the individual beings are complementary. When we as individuals are ready to live divinely in our earth-home, and when earth is fully ready to receive us and welcome us as members of its family, then God's choicest Blessings are bound to shower on our devoted heads and on earth's devoted heart.

AN OVERVIEW OF SRI CHINMOY'S CONTRIBUTIONS TO WORLD PEACE

For over thirty years, Sri Chinmoy has tirelessly dedicated his life to the pursuit of world peace and to the fulfillment of the unlimited potential of the human spirit.

A prolific author, poet, artist, musician, an enthusiastic athlete, and a treasured spiritual guide, he has inspired millions of people the world over to discover the wellspring of peace and fulfillment that lies deep within each of us.

Sri Chinmoy: The Peace Meditation at the United Nations

- For a quarter of a century, Sri Chinmoy has offered his devoted service to the highest ideals of the United Nations through twice weekly meditations for delegates and staff.

- The Meditation Group offers distinguished members of the international community the U Thant Peace Award for contributions to world peace carried out in the spirit of the late Secretary-General. Recipients of the Award include former Soviet President and Nobel Peace Prize Laureate Mikhail Gorbachev, Nobel Peace Prize Laureate Mother Teresa and UNICEF Executive Director James Grant.
- The Meditation Group has also sponsored many special events, including commemorative programs in honor of inspirational figures such as John F. Kennedy, Dr. Martin Luther King, Jr. and Dag Hammarskjöld.
- In cooperation with a number of Permanent Representatives of the U.N. Member States, the Meditation Group sponsors several special events each year, including: "peace walks" commemorating United Nations Charter Day (June 26th) and United Nations Day (October 24th); a walk for peace on the first day of the General Assembly, followed by an interdenominational prayer breakfast; "Seven Minutes of World Peace," a simultaneous global observance of peaceful silence in honor of U.N. Day; an 18.5-mile relay run from the site of the former U.N. Headquarters in Lake Success, NY, to the current headquarters in Manhattan; and one-mile peace runs in the U.N. Garden for delegates and staff.

Meetings with World Leaders

- In his ongoing efforts to foster harmony around the world, Sri Chinmoy has had heartfelt discussions on world peace with heads of state, religious leaders and luminaries from many fields, including Pope John Paul II, Mikhail Gorbachev, Mother Teresa, Vaclav Havel and Nelson Mandela.

Literature

- In over 1,100 books of poetry, prose, essays, stories and plays, Sri Chinmoy conveys the richness and diversity of the quest for peace and self-understanding. His works have been translated into 15 languages.
- Among his literary works, Sri Chinmoy has written 50,000 poems, including *10,000 Flower-Flames*, a 100-volume work, and *27,000 Aspiration Plants*, a 270-volume work of which 220 have been completed.
- Sri Chinmoy has offered over 850 lectures, 200 of them at universities worldwide.

Music

- Sri Chinmoy has offered over 400 Peace Concerts and public meditations worldwide, always free of charge.
- Half a million people around the world have joined Sri Chinmoy in a deep inner experience of peace.
- The Peace Concerts have been offered to full houses at some of the world's most prestigious venues, including Avery Fisher Hall and Carnegie Hall in New York, the Royal Albert Hall in London, the Great Hall of the Australian National Parliament in Canberra, and Louise Davies Hall in San Francisco.
- Sri Chinmoy has composed 13,000 songs which explore the length and breadth of the search for self-discovery, and regularly performs them in concert on dozens of different instruments.
- Sri Chinmoy plays over 100 different musical instruments, including harmonium, esraj, flute, cello, piano and organ.
- Among the songs Sri Chinmoy has composed, hundreds have been dedicated to individuals and nations.

Art

- Since 1974, Sri Chinmoy has painted more than 15,000 acrylics and watercolors that have been displayed in galleries worldwide.
- In the span of four years, Sri Chinmoy has completed a series of four million soul-bird drawings entitled "Four Million Dream-Freedom-Peace-Birds"—the bird being a symbol of the peace and freedom we all cherish.
- The soul-bird drawings have been exhibited at locations such as UNESCO, the Senate Foyer at the Parliament House in Canberra, the Mall Gallery in London, the International Arrivals Building at JFK Airport in New York, and Peace Osaka Hall in Japan.

Sri Chinmoy Oneness-Home Peace Run

- Since 1987, the biennial Sri Chinmoy Oneness-Home Peace run, an international torch relay run, had brought together millions of people in the spirit of friendship and harmony.
- Passing a flaming peace torch from hand to hand and heart to heart, the Peace Run has covered nearly 200,000 miles in 80 countries on all seven continents.
- The Peace Run has received the enthusiastic participation and endorsement of leaders and luminaries worldwide, including Pope John Paul II, Mikhail Gorbachev, Mother Teresa, Queen Elizabeth II of the United Kingdom, Chancellor Kohl of Germany, Archbishop Desmond Tutu and the Dalai Lama.
- In 1991 the Peace Run was the inspiration behind the first-ever relay between Egypt and Israel, and in 1993 the first-ever relay between Jordan and Israel.
- In 1995 four Peace Torches lit an eternal flame of peace at the 50th Anniversary celebrations of the end of World War II in Europe. The Peace Torches also lit Queen

Elizabeth's torch, with which she ignited the first of 1,800 beacons of peace throughout Great Britain.

Sri Chinmoy Peace-Blossoms

- An international family of over 800 significant landmarks in 50 nations dedicated as daily reminders of our need for peace.
- Commemorative plaques provide inspiration to millions of passersby each year, and designate the Peace-Blossom—as a Sri Chinmoy Peace Falls, for example—in honor of Sri Chinmoy's global peace-vision.
- The Sri Chinmoy Peace-Blossoms family includes some of the world's most precious natural wonders:
  - Niagara Falls
  - the Matterhorn
  - Langtang II, a 6,751m unclimbed peak in the Himalayas
  - the tallest mountains in ten countries
  - Lake Baikal, the world's oldest and deepest freshwater lake
  - Manitoulin Island, the largest freshwater island in the world
- The Sri Chinmoy Peace-Blossoms family also includes the national capitals of Canada, Australia, New Zealand, Iceland, Scotland and Fiji; 13 states and hundreds of cities and towns in America; the University of Cincinnati; bridges joining a dozen nations; and the entire 200km border between Norway and Russia.

Athletics

- Sri Chinmoy has completed 21 marathons, 5 ultramarathons, 200 road races and nearly 50 100m races.
- In a dramatic demonstration of the indomitable power of the human spirit, Sri Chinmoy has performed several historic feats of strength, including:

- Lifting 7,063 lbs. with his right arm at the age of 55, after only one year and seven months of weight training. A year and a half later, he lifted 7,040 lbs. with his left arm.
- Lifting 2,038 lbs. using a standard calf-raise machine, having begun his calf-raise training less than six months earlier with 400 lbs.
- Lifting his own body weight of 150 lbs. with one arm, a total of 150 times in 11 minutes 13 seconds.
- In over 500 athletic events worldwide each year, the Sri Chinmoy Marathon Team brings people of all ages and nations together in sport, from two-mile fun runs to masters track and field competitions, to the world's longest certified race of 1,300 miles.

Lifting Up the World with a Oneness-Heart

- A unique award program offered by Sri Chinmoy to recognize individuals from all walks of life who, by excelling in their respective fields of endeavor, have inspired and uplifted humanity.
- Utilizing a specially constructed platform, Sri Chinmoy actually lifts the honorees overhead with one arm before presenting them with a special "Lifting Up the World" medallion.
- To date, over 2,000 individuals around the globe have been honored in a spirit of oneness and appreciation for their diverse achievements. Honorees include heads of state, diplomats, spiritual leaders of many faiths, Nobel Laureates, members of the academic community, performing artists and world-class athletes.

Global Meditations for Inner and Outer Peace

- In addition to meditations at the United Nations, Sri Chinmoy had offered silent meditations for peace at the